Historical American Biographies

GEORGE EASTMAN

Bringing Photography to the People

Lynda Pflueger

Enslow Publishers, Inc.

40 Industrial Road   PO Box 38
Box 398   Aldershot
Berkeley Heights, NJ 07922 Hants GU12 6BP
USA   UK

http://www.enslow.com

Dedication
To Dawn, Dave, Aaron, Noah, and Isaac Berg,
for all their loving support.

Library of Congress Cataloging-in-Publication Data

Pflueger, Lynda.
    George Eastman: bringing photography to the people / Lynda Pflueger.
       p. cm. — (Historical American biographies)
    Includes bibliographical references and index.
    Summary: Follows the life and career of the man who revolutionized
    photography by developing a camera simple enough for anyone to use.
    ISBN 0-7660-1617-X
      1. Eastman, George, 1854-1932—Juvenile literature. 2.
Photographers—United States—Biography—Juvenile literature. [1.
Eastman, George, 1854-1932. 2. Inventors. 3. Photography—History.] I.
Title. II. Series.
TR140.E3 P45 2001
770'.92—dc21
                                 2001003401

Printed in the United States of America

10 9 8 7 6 5 4 3 2 1

To Our Readers: We have done our best to make sure all Internet addresses in this book were active and appropriate when we went to press. However, the author and the publisher have no control over and assume no liability for the material available on those Internet sites or on other Web sites they may link to. Any comments or suggestions can be sent by e-mail to comments@enslow.com or to the address on the back cover.

Illustration Credits: Courtesy George Eastman House, pp. 7, 64, 89; Department of Rare Books and Special Collections, University of Rochester Library, pp. 14, 40, 58, 95, 100, 105, 108; Enslow Publishers, Inc., pp. 16, 97, 102; Lynda Pflueger, pp. 13, 56, 62; National Archives & Records Administration, pp. 4, 104, 110; Reproduced from the *Dictionary of American Portraits*, Published by Dover Publications, Inc., in 1967, pp. 36, 73.

Cover Illustration: Department of Rare Books and Special Collections, University of Rochester Library (Background); Reproduced from the *Dictionary of American Portraits*, Published by Dover Publications, Inc., in 1967 (Eastman Portrait).

CONTENTS

George Eastman

1

AMATEUR

In the late 1870s, Rochester, New York, was a prosperous, booming community. Business was good. Most of the wheat grown in western New York was shipped down the Erie Canal to be ground into flour in Rochester's mills. Wagons, trains, and boats were used to ship shoes, clothing, furniture, tools, and other goods made in Rochester to markets around the world.

In this prosperous climate, many businessmen were investing in real estate. George Eastman, a twenty-four-year-old bank clerk at Rochester Savings Bank, became aware of investment opportunities in Santo Domingo, the capital city of the

Dominican Republic in the Caribbean Sea. At the time, President Ulysses S. Grant was considering purchasing Samana Bay, the Santo Domingo harbor, to establish a U.S. naval base there.

Eastman wanted to expand his real estate investments.[1] He was curious about what the land looked like in Santo Domingo and what kind of return he could get on his money. He decided to take a vacation and visit the city.

One of Eastman's friends, a fellow bank employee, suggested that he record his trip with a camera. Eastman liked the idea and purchased a photographic outfit for $94.26, the equivalent of nearly five weeks' wages. The equipment consisted of a huge camera, a tripod, a plate holder, a nitrate bath, jars, dishes, a funnel, brushes, chemicals, and a tent to use as a darkroom.[2]

From the beginning, the cumbersome photographic equipment bothered Eastman. "The bulk of the paraphernalia worried me," he said. "It seemed that one ought to be able to carry less than a pack-horse load."[3]

The wet-plate process used to make photographs was also complicated. First, a glass plate was coated with a sticky, transparent substance called collodion. While the glass plate was still wet, it was taken into a dark room and dipped in a solution of silver nitrate. This made the plate sensitive to light. Then,

George Eastman's first photograph, taken in October 1877, was of the Genesee River in Rochester, New York.

while still in the darkroom, the plate was inserted into a lightproof plate holder. At this point, the plate holder was taken out of the darkroom and placed inside the camera. In order to take a photograph, the cover was slid off the glass plate holder (inside the camera) and the lens cap removed from the camera. Once exposed and before it had time to dry, the glass plate was taken back to the darkroom, developed into a negative, and treated with a fixing agent. Eastman experimented with the wet-plate process, but made little progress until he took lessons from two local photographers.

Eventually, Eastman canceled his plans to visit Santo Domingo. "But that did not matter so much," he later admitted, "because, in making ready [for the trip] I became wholly absorbed in photography."[4] He took more lessons and read photographic journals. When he had the chance, he went on trips to practice his hobby.

During the summer of 1878, he traveled to Mackinac Island on Lake Huron in Michigan. He was interested in photographing a natural bridge that had formed on the island. While he was setting up his equipment, a group of tourists spotted him. They thought he was a professional photographer and lingered near the bridge so he would take their photograph.

Eastman ignored them and went about taking his photographs. When he finished developing his plates, one of the men from the group approached him to inquire about the cost of his photographs. Eastman told him he was an amateur and his photographs were not for sale.

The tourist became angry and complained, "Then why did you let us stand in the hot sun for a full half-hour while you fooled around with your contraptions? You ought to wear a sign saying that you are an amateur!"[5] The tourist had no idea that one day this young amateur would revolutionize the field of photography by making it accessible to everyone and the camera as convenient to use as a pencil.[6]

2

EARLY YEARS

George Eastman was the fourth child of George Washington Eastman, born September 9, 1815, and Maria Kilbourn, born on August 22, 1821. His parents were the youngest members of their large families. The Eastmans had ten children and the Kilbourns seven.[1] Both families lived on farms in central New York near Waterville.

George Washington (G. W.) Eastman attended school at the Hamilton Academy. He had excellent penmanship and turned his skill into a profession by establishing a business college, the Eastman Commercial College, in Rochester, New York. The school offered courses in penmanship, bookkeeping, and spelling.

Underground Railroad

The Eastmans' farm was a stop on the Underground Railroad. In their barn, a special carriage was always ready to sneak a runaway slave to freedom in Canada in the middle of the night.[2]

The Underground Railroad was run by a group of people who did not believe in slavery. Railroad terms were used to describe the network's secret operations. The operators of the network were called "conductors," their houses "stations," and the slaves they guided "freight." The routes from safe house to safe house were also called "lines."

Maria Kilbourn, whose first name was pronounced "Mah-rye-ah," was unusually well educated for a woman of her time. She attended the Vernon Academy and then Kellogg's Seminary, where her instructors were young ministers. She studied philosophy, chemistry, rhetoric, astronomy, and botany. Both schools supported abolitionist causes. Maria belonged to a sewing society that made clothes for a colony of runaway slaves in Toronto, Canada.

G. W. Eastman and Maria were childhood playmates. In 1836, G. W. Eastman's brother, Almon, married Maria's sister, Sophia. Six years later, both George and Maria were visiting their older siblings in Kingsville, Ohio. At the time, Maria wrote to friends complaining that everyone else was getting married and that she had found no "congenial company" while visiting her sister, except G. W. Eastman.[3]

Two years later, on September 25, 1844, G. W. Eastman and Maria were married. The couple made their home in Rochester. On November 4, 1845, their first child was born, a daughter they named Ellen Maria. In the family Bible, her arrival was recorded as a gift from G. W. Eastman to his wife for New Year's.[4]

Waterville

Four years later, the family moved to a small, ten-acre farm near Waterville. G. W. Eastman commuted regularly between his family in Waterville and his business in Rochester, a hundred miles away. In 1850, their second child, Emma Kate, was born. At the age of fourteen months, she came down with polio, which left her with a crippled arm, wrist, and foot.

While his family was growing, G. W. Eastman expanded his successful business school and wrote several textbooks. He also purchased additional acres adjoining his family's farm and opened a nursery. The grounds were filled with fruit trees, roses, and ornamental shrubs. In 1852, their third child was born, but he died shortly after birth.[5] Two years later, their fourth child, George Eastman, was born on July 12, 1854.

George Eastman's boyhood home in Waterville, New York

George was a well-behaved child. His older sister Ellen Maria often wheeled him downtown in his carriage while she did their father's banking. Their father believed that the only way to bring up responsible children was to let them "learn by actual experience," which was the same teaching philosophy he used in his business school.[6]

Return to Rochester

In 1858, George's father became ill and put his property in Waterville up for sale. It did not sell quickly, so it was not until 1860 that the family moved to Rochester. The *Rochester Union and Advertiser* newspaper welcomed the family back, commenting that G. W. Eastman was a qualified teacher and managed one of the finest business colleges of his time.[7] On May 2, 1862, the same newspaper reported his death from a brain disorder.

Two months before his eighth birthday, George Eastman's world was turned upside down. His father's death left his family without an income. In order to support her family, his mother took in boarders.

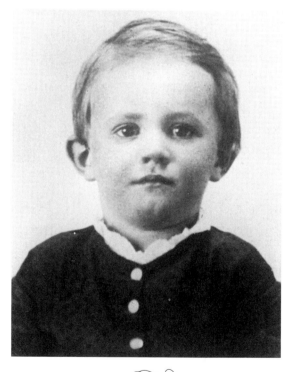

This is the first photograph of George Eastman.

Work and Ledgers

In 1868, Cornelius Waydell, a well-known insurance agent, offered fourteen-year-old George a job and he dropped out of school to take it. At the time, many children dropped out of school in order to help support their families. From 8:00 A.M. to 6:00 P.M. every day of the week except Sunday, George swept Waydell's office, ran errands, cleaned off desks, added wood to the stove, and emptied spittoons—containers for people to spit in. He earned three dollars per week and was delighted to be a man of "independent means."[8]

George believed, as his father had, that people should not trust financial transactions to "memory alone."[9] He kept a ledger in which he documented his income and expenses. In 1868, he earned $131 and spent $39 on clothes and paid his mother $22.22 for room and board. He also spent $16.35 on items such as ice cream on his birthday, $8.05 on shoes, $3.03 on underwear, and $3.35 on hats. After his expenditures, he had $39 left of his income for the year.

Shortly after George left school to go to work, his older sister Ellen married George Worthington Andrus in the Eastman living room. He gave his sister a lady's parasol, as a wedding gift.[10] The couple moved to Cleveland, Ohio. George found his brother-in-law to be loud and vulgar.

In 1869, George's salary was increased to four

dollars per week and he earned $233 that year. The following year, Waydell failed to give George another raise, so he quit and went to work for a rival insurance company, Buell & Brewster. In a short time, George received two raises and his salary increased to $35 a month. During the year, George studied French, attended lectures, became interested in stereographic photographs, bought coal for his mother's home, and paid one of his mother's doctor bills.

George always shared his Christmas and birthday gifts with his crippled sister, Katy. He also worried

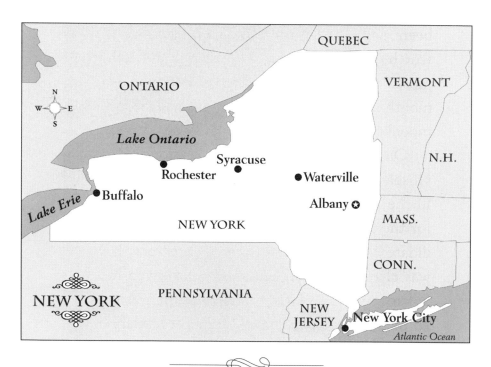

George Eastman was born in Waterville, New York. In 1860, his family moved to Rochester.

about her health. She was confined to a wheelchair and was susceptible to many illnesses. When the weather turned cold, she had to stay home from school and recite her lessons to their mother. On December 3, 1870, she became ill and died. George bought a new suit to wear to her funeral and paid to have her coffin taken to Waterville, where she was buried next to their father.

In 1871, a fire in Chicago brought in so much business to Buell & Brewster that even the firm's young clerks were needed to write policies. George bragged in a letter to one of his cousins that he had been permitted to write new insurance polices worth "three-quarters of a million dollars or more."[11] At the time, George was earning $41.66 a month at the insurance company and $8 a month moonlighting as a Rochester fireman.

One of Maria Eastman's boarders, Thomas Husband, told Eastman about a banking job at Rochester Savings Bank in 1874. Eastman applied for the job and was selected from seven other candidates by the bank's board of directors. His title was clerk and he earned a salary of seven hundred dollars per year. Nine months later, he was promoted to second assistant bookkeeper at a salary of one thousand dollars per year, an excellent salary for a twenty-one-year-old at the time.[12]

3

INVENTOR

While working at the savings bank, George Eastman became fascinated with photography. He bought a camera and began experimenting with the wet-plate process. In 1878, he found an article in the *British Journal of Photography* that contained a formula for a dry-plate emulsion in which glass plates could be coated and used dry. The idea intrigued him. Even though he had dropped out of school and never studied chemistry, he began experimenting.

After working at the bank during the day, he went home and cooked emulsion formulas on his mother's kitchen stove. Then he baked the plates in the oven and tested them by taking photographs of his neighbors' houses across the street. He worked late into the night and often slept fully clothed on the kitchen floor. He became as "thin as pie crust" and his mother began to worry about his health.[1]

Eastman found that he "could tell by the color" of an emulsion "whether it was approaching the point where it had cooked enough." Then he "could estimate how long it would take to finish" and lie down and sleep "for a few hours." He always woke up in time and never spoiled a batch.[2]

His progress was slow. After many experiments, Eastman finally came "upon a coating of gelatine and silver bromide that had all the necessary photographic qualities" he was looking for.[3] Nevertheless, the process of coating the plates by hand was slow and tedious. Eastman had to pour the hot emulsion from a teakettle onto the glass plate, then spread it with a rod.

He knew there had to be a better way. So he designed a machine that would mechanically coat the plates. His plate coater looked like a large stamp wetter, a machine used to moisten the adhesive on the backs of postage stamps. Inside a trough, a roller turned, dipping into emulsion. Glass plates were pulled across the roller while being held above the apparatus by suction cups. Eastman was confident that nobody would want to coat his or her own photographic plates by hand after seeing his invention.

At first, Eastman considered photography a hobby. He only wanted to simplify the process for himself. He soon realized, however, that selling ready-to-use photographic plates might be a profitable business endeavor. In 1879, he decided to take the risk and go into business. He withdrew four hundred dollars from his savings account and sailed to England aboard the *Abyssinia* to obtain a patent for his plate-coating machine. At the time, London was the financial and photographic center of the world.

When Eastman returned home after receiving his English patent, he hired George B. Selden, one of his former photography tutors, to obtain a patent for the plate-coating machine in the United States.

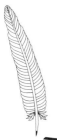

Patents

A patent is a document issued by a government agency giving the applicant exclusive rights to make or use an invention. The owner of a patent has the right to prevent others from producing, selling, or using an invention in the country where the patent was issued.

Frederick Scott Archer, the Englishman who invented the wet-plate process, did not obtain a patent. His highly successful invention revolutionized photography, but without the protection of a patent, he died at the age of forty-four, leaving his wife and children penniless. George Eastman may have been aware of this tragedy. He always protected his own inventions with patents.

Selden, an attorney, filed the application for Patent
No. 226,503 on September 9, 1879, and the patent
was issued on April 13, 1880.

The "Biz"

While setting up his business, Eastman wrote to his
mother, who was away visiting relatives. He told her
he was about to take the plunge and go into business
for himself. He called the new adventure his "biz."[4]

The "biz" turned out to be a one-man show. In
April 1880, Eastman rented a room above a music
store in the Martin Building at 73 State Street, just
two blocks from his bank job. After work each day,
he rode his bicycle to his factory and worked late
into the night. He cooked the emulsions, coated the
plates, boxed the plates for shipment, and kept
the books. He designed and hung a hammock in the
corner of the room where he could take naps
between stirring batches of emulsion.[5]

Business was slow at first. However, one of
Eastman's former teachers, George Monroe, was
impressed with Eastman's dry plates. He showed
them to Edward Anthony, one of the owners of
E. & H. T. Anthony of New York City, the largest
supply house of photographic materials in the
United States. A few months later, Anthony
ordered $1,053.08 worth of dry plates.

Eastman Dry-Plate Company

On December 1880, Eastman formed a partnership with an old family friend, Henry Strong, who invested one thousand dollars in the business. They signed a contract and the Eastman Dry-Plate Company was born. Strong became the president and Eastman the treasurer.

Strong, a buggy whip manufacturer, was a personable, gregarious businessman who loved to take risks. For a short time, Strong and his family had boarded with the Eastmans after the Strongs' house burned down. He had become fond of Eastman and said, "I have great faith in that young man."[6] Eastman was impressed with Strong's business successes. He called him "a bully old boy" and added, "I love him from the bottom of my heart."[7]

Business was good. In a short time, the company expanded and moved into a third-floor loft in the same building on State Street. Eastman hired a supervisor to coat plates while he worked at the bank. By March 1881, the Eastman Dry-Plate Company had six employees—a salesman, a bookkeeper, two packers, and two women to coat the plates. By the end of the year, the company employed sixteen workers. Monthly sales averaged four thousand dollars.

Eastman, who had promised his mother that he would make it up to her for everything she had suffered after his father died, was now making a comfortable living. He earned fifteen hundred dollars a year working at the bank. His mother no longer needed to take in boarders. They lived in a house at 49 Jones Avenue and could afford a cook and a part-time handyman to take care of things around the house.

Even though his business was a financial success, Eastman did not plan to quit his bank job. In September 1881, he changed his mind when he was passed over for a promotion in favor of a relative of one of the bank directors. This type of favoritism offended Eastman, and he resigned. He felt it was a great injustice, neither fair nor right.[8]

Dry Plates Fail

Shortly after he left his bank job, a disaster hit. Dealers began to complain that the Eastman dry plates were failing. They either registered no image when exposed to light or were fogged over. Eastman went to Anthony's store in New York to investigate. At first, he thought the age of the plates might be the problem, but he discovered that both old and new plates were bad. He could not figure out what had happened. For two years, the plates had been good. Now, Eastman had no choice but to recall all the plates and take the loss.

Determined to solve the problem, he returned to Rochester, shut down his factory, and began round-the-clock testing. After 454 attempts of mixing and remixing batches of emulsions, he had made little progress. In his notebook he wrote: "Trials show slight red fog & slight veil."[9] He made eighteen more unsuccessful tests and was still baffled.

Time was running out. He had purchased a lot on the corner of State and Vought Streets in Rochester and hired a contractor to build a new four-story building to house his factory. When Eastman's creditors became anxious to be paid, the contractor wanted to foreclose on the property. Eastman, along with Strong and their attorney, convinced him to wait.

In a final attempt to resolve the problem, Eastman, Henry Strong, and their emulsion assistant, Walter Butler, sailed for England on board the *Germanic* on March 11, 1882. In London, they found the answer to their puzzle. Their English supplier of gelatin had changed its source without notifying customers. On April 4, the three men returned to Rochester, and after sixteen experiments, Eastman once again had dry plates that were "clear and good."[10]

Eastman borrowed six hundred dollars to reopen his factory and signed a note promising to repay the money in ten days. He cut the price of his plates 25 percent to encourage his customers to return. Eastman later recalled, "when the plates fogged it was a terrible experience—like waking in the morning with a clear mind and paralysis in every muscle."[11]

From this experience, Eastman learned to test all chemicals and ingredients before he used them. By the end of the year, business had turned around and the Eastman Dry-Plate Company made a profit of $14,889.99. Providing *"good goods"* was a key to Eastman's success.[12] Unlike his competitors, Eastman put his profits back into his company and continued to experiment.

Film

Eastman's next challenge was to find a substitute for glass plate negatives. He wanted a lighter, rollable substance and began experimenting with paper and collodion, a moist, sticky substance also used in the wet-plate process. His first experiments were successful, but the graininess of the paper showed through.

After several more experiments, Eastman tried treating paper with hot castor oil and glycerin to smooth over the graininess of the paper. Then he coated the paper with collodion, applied a layer of gelatin, followed by a layer of photographic emulsion. After exposing the paper plate to light to capture an image, he soaked it in a hot bath to dissolve the gelatin, leaving a film negative.

Eastman called his new invention American Film. He patented the film and the process he developed to sensitize large rolls of paper with photographic emulsions. This was the first time photographic film had been produced in continuous strips. Since stripping the film from its paper backing was a tricky operation, Eastman opened a film-developing department so that amateur photographers would not have to develop their film themselves.

Roll Holder

While perfecting his new film, Eastman became aware of William Walker, a camera designer and manufacturer. Walker had designed and marketed a small camera that had interchangeable parts called Walker's Pocket Camera. Eastman was impressed with Walker's ideas. Because the camera had interchangeable parts, it could easily be mass-produced in a factory. When Walker's company folded, Eastman offered him a small salary and stock options to join his company. Walker became Eastman's second partner.

Walker's assignment was to develop a new mechanism to hold the paper-backed film Eastman had developed. In a short time, Walker created a

Partners

George Eastman, Henry Strong, and William Walker were an odd combination of personalities. Eastman, an introvert, was shy and often uncomfortable in social situations. Strong, an extrovert, was friendly and happy-go-lucky. He often represented the company at social functions. Walker was a pessimist. He rarely looked on the bright side of things and loved to complain.

lightweight wooden frame to which two spools were attached, one at each end. The paper film was wrapped around one spool and then fed over the frame to the second spool as each photograph was taken. A turn key on the side of the camera advanced the film. There were twenty-four exposures on each roll of film, and the roller holder could be fitted to the back of any standard camera.

Excited about his new film system, Eastman bragged that his company was "ready to scoop the world in the next few weeks."[13] He felt he was leading the way to revolutionize the field of photography and he wanted "to popularize" it to an extent that had scarcely been "dreamed of."[14]

In September 1884, Eastman announced that he was about to introduce a new process that would replace photographic glass plates and "save

Photographers about a quarter of a million dollars yearly . . ."[15]

Eastman changed the name of his company to Eastman Dry-Plate and Film Company and sent Walker to Europe to set up a branch office in London. A few months later, he entered his new film system, which he described as a complete system of film photography, in the London International Inventions Exhibition and won a gold medal.

The *British Journal of Photography* wrote a favorable article about Eastman's invention and suggested that all serious photographers examine "the ingenious mechanism." Eastman also entered his invention in several other European exhibits and won awards.[16]

Sister's Death

Even with his successes, 1884 ended on a sad note for Eastman. His older sister, Ellen, died. After her death, her thirteen-year-old daughter, Ellen Andrus, came to live with her grandmother and uncle Eastman for nearly a year. Her brother Royal often visited during school vacations. Eastman liked to photograph Ellen and Royal clowning around in his backyard.

4

BUSINESSMAN

Despite awards and favorable publicity, Eastman's new film system was not well received Many professional photographers were set in their ways and reluctant to change. "When we started out with our scheme of film photography," Eastman wrote, "we expected that everybody that used glass plates would take up films, but we found that in order to make a large business we would have to reach the general public and create a new class of patrons [customers]."[1] Eastman met this challenge by continuing to perfect his rollable film and developing a lightweight, inexpensive, handheld camera.

Chemist

In 1886, Eastman searched for an expert to continue experimenting with film solutions. He contacted Dr. Samuel A. Lattimore, head of the chemistry department at the University of Rochester, and asked him to recommend a chemist. Lattimore suggested his undergraduate assistant, Henry Reichenbach.

In August, Eastman hired Reichenbach, whom he considered an "ingenious, quick-witted fellow," to dedicate his time to chemical experiments.[2] This was one of the first times an American manufacturer had hired a trained chemist to devote all of his time to chemical research.[3] Eastman gave Reichenbach two assignments: to improve the speed and sensitivity of his photographic emulsions and to find a strong, transparent material to replace paper as the film base.[4] Even though Reichenbach knew nothing about photography, he took on his assignment with "enthusiasm and skill."[5]

While Reichenbach experimented with emulsions, Eastman turned his attention to advertising and promotion. He wrote all the advertising copy, decided where to place advertisements, and personally chose and trained all his salesmen. Before a salesman was hired, he had to pass a handwriting test and a personal interview with Eastman.

Workaholic

Eastman was a workaholic. He had time for nothing but work. Many nights he slept in a hammock and cooked his own meals at the factory. Often, his mother would come down to take him home for "a square meal and a good night's rest."[6]

Eastman relied a great deal on his mother. He always discussed his business problems with her. He once said she had "uncanny judgment in business matters" and if she vetoed something, she was always right.[7]

Eastman's First Camera

In October 1887, Eastman began working on a model for an inexpensive, handheld camera. He commissioned three Rochester companies to build the main parts. Frank Brownell's cabinet and camera shop built the wooden frame. Yawman & Erbe's machinist shop produced the camera's shutter. Bausch & Lomb, an optical company that produced lenses for glasses, made the camera's lens.

The leather-covered camera weighed 22 ounces and was 6 3/4 inches long, 3 3/4 inches wide, and 3 3/4 inches high. It looked like a small black shoebox and cost twenty-five dollars. The camera came with its own carrying case with a shoulder strap, and enough film to take one hundred photographs. When all the pictures were taken, the camera was sent back to Rochester. For ten dollars, the film was developed and a new spool of film was inserted into the camera. Then the printed photographs and the camera were mailed back to the customer.

Kodak

Eastman named his new camera Kodak. "I devised the name myself," Eastman later commented. "The letter 'K' had been a favorite with me—it seemed a strong, incisive [sharp, keen, and penetrating] sort of letter. . . ."[8] Eastman tried various combinations of the letter until he finally came up with a word that was short, pronounced the same way in every language, and not associated previously with anything in the field of photography.

In May 1888, the first Kodak camera was sold. Two months later, twenty-five Kodak cameras were displayed at the convention of the Photographer's Association of America held in Minneapolis, Minnesota. One photographer who attended the affair commented to his peers that Eastman had "the cutest little trick box of a camera he calls a Kodak."[9] Eastman's camera won first prize in the camera competition. On his way home, after attending the convention, Eastman stopped in Cleveland and gave his niece Ellen Andrus a Kodak camera so that she could go on to become arguably the best photographer in the family.[10] Ellen was a natural when it came to photography. She knew how to choose subjects and compose shots.

Customer Service

Eastman realized the importance of having satisfied customers. His camera came with a written guarantee and a manual. At first, Eastman hired a professional writer to create the manual, but he was dissatisfied with the results. He felt that the writer had "utterly ignored" the simplicity of the camera's operation.[11] He fired the writer, sat down, and in less than five hours wrote the manual himself. In the manual Eastman explained that, "for twenty years the art of photography stood still. . . . Four years ago the amateur photographer was confined to heavy glass plates for making his negatives. . . . Today photography has been reduced to a cycle of three operations."[12] These three operations, or steps, were: Pull the string, press the button, and turn the key. A few months later, Eastman condensed these instructions into a catchy slogan: "You push the button, and we do the rest."[13]

In less than a year, thirteen thousand Kodak cameras had been sold and up to seventy rolls of film were being processed by the company every day.[14] The demand was so great that Eastman was afraid his company might be mobbed. Letters testifying to the pleasure of using a Kodak camera poured into the company office:

> I believe this is the first camera that has ever been brought on the market that could be put in an ordinary man's hand and expect to get results.
>
> It is the greatest boon on earth to the traveling man, like myself, to be able to bring home, at so small an outlay of time and money, a complete photographic memorandum of his travels . . . [it] . . . will be my constant companion.
>
> My first hundred pictures are highly satisfactory. Their excellence and beauty surpassed my hopes. . . .[15]

Transparent Film

Shortly after the first Kodak cameras were produced, Reichenbach had made great progress in developing a flexible, transparent film. The new film had a nitrocellulose backing instead of paper, which eliminated the need to strip the film negative from its base before developing. Anticipating his chemist's success, Eastman developed a way to mass-produce the film. Under his direction, twelve film-coating tables were created by cementing together three and a half-foot-wide sheets of glass to form eighty-foot-long tables. The joints, where the pieces of glass met, were ground and polished to create a long, silky, and smooth surface.

After the nitrocellulose backing, or "dope," as it was commonly called, was spread on the long coating tables, air ducts were opened above the tables. Warm air flowed into the room, drying the nitrocellulose mixture. The next day, the lights were turned off in the coating room and a light-sensitive photographic emulsion was spread over the hardened dope. Once again, the film was dried with warm air. A few hours later, it was peeled off the glass tables, cut into strips, rolled onto spools, and placed in light-tight containers.

In April 1889, Eastman filed a patent application for his transparent film and the process he used to create it. The patent examiner determined that Eastman's application was similar to a patent application previously filed in 1877 by Reverend Hannibal Goodwin of Newark, New Jersey. Goodwin's patent request had been denied because the description of his process had been too broad. Goodwin had been advised to amend his application, but he never followed through. Due to this fact, on December 10, 1889, Eastman was issued patent number 417,202 for his transparent film. Although Eastman's and Goodwin's formulas were not identical, their similarities would later come back to haunt Eastman.

When production of his transparent film began, Eastman wrote to Walker, who was in London, and reported that the new film "is the 'slickest' product that we ever tried to make and the method of manufacture will eliminate all of the defects hither-to experienced in film manufacture."[16] Eastman felt the market for his new product would be enormous.

Motion Pictures

Eastman's transparent film made the development of motion pictures possible. Thomas Alva Edison,

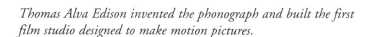

Thomas Alva Edison invented the phonograph and built the first film studio designed to make motion pictures.

Kinetoscope

Edison invented the first motion picture machine, called a Kinetoscope. The word Kinetoscope comes from two Greek words: *kineto*, which means "movement," and *scopos*, which means "to watch." The machine consisted of a cabinet containing a peephole and a phonograph. A customer would look through the peephole at a short motion picture and listen to the phonograph through two rubber ear tubes that were attached to the machine. The moving pictures and the sound from the phonograph were synchronized by a belt that connected them.

who invented the phonograph, was also interested in photography of motion. Edison had begun experimenting with an apparatus that would do for the eye what the phonograph had done for the ear.

Previously, Edison had recorded a series of images on film and then played them back in rapid succession. This made the images look like they were moving. The film he used had been of poor quality and ripped easily. When Edison examined Eastman's new transparent film, he supposedly shouted to his staff, "That's it.—Now work like hell!"[17]

Return to England

In July 1889, Eastman traveled to England to apply for film patents and investigate expanding his factory in London. His mother accompanied him. While they were in London, Walker introduced them to two fellow Americans, George and Josephine Dickman, at a dinner party. Dickman was an experienced international businessman and his wife, Josephine, was a trained singer. A friendship quickly developed between Eastman, his sixty-eight-year-old mother, and the charming international couple.

On weekends, Eastman escorted his mother to art galleries, museums, and the theater. During the week, Josephine Dickman took over and entertained Mrs. Eastman. She also accompanied George Eastman on shopping trips where he bought gloves and hats for himself, china and silver for his home, and pieces of jewelry for his mother. Eastman later wrote that the trip to Europe did "a world of good" for his mother.[18]

Before Eastman returned home, he instructed Walker to find land on the outskirts of London to build a new manufacturing plant. He told Walker they needed ten acres of grassland "where there is no dust, no smoke, good water, good drainage . . ." Eastman wanted the factory started within nine to ten months.[19]

New Rochester Plant

A larger factory was also needed in Rochester. Dust, smoke, and lack of space were seriously hampering the manufacturing of film. Eastman asked one of his board members, Brackett Clark, to look into the matter. Several pieces of property were investigated. The most promising was farmland in the nearby town of Greece along Charlotte Boulevard. Greece was a rural community located just three miles from Eastman's current office on State Street in downtown Rochester.

When it was learned that the fourteen-acre site could provide an adequate supply of water, one of the main requirements for manufacturing film, Eastman bought the property for $22,800. On October 1, 1890, a groundbreaking ceremony was held. Three buildings were constructed on the site: a power plant, a film factory, and a testing laboratory. Electric lights and motors were installed in the film factory, and the emulsion room was air-conditioned by a fifty-ton ice machine.[20] Six months after the three buildings were completed, plans were being made for additional buildings.

The grounds of the new factory were professionally landscaped with brick pavements and numerous plants and shrubs. Fresh flowers from the grounds were often sent to Eastman's office. In time, the

When he was thirty-six years old, George Eastman had this portrait taken in Paris, France.

factory site became known as Kodak Park and was one of the first industrial parks in America.

Uptown

Due to his success, Eastman decided it was time to move to a more fashionable part of town. He sublet a fifteen-room house in Arnold Park, a newer section of Rochester, for twelve hundred dollars a year. Eastman's frugal mother thought moving was a frivolous idea. She wanted to stay in her old neighborhood with her friends. Eastman told her that they "had better begin to enjoy" their money or they would not "get the full benefit of it."[21] Then he left for Europe, leaving her to take charge of the move.

Maria Eastman had no choice but to move. She did not make it easy on her son, though. At first, she wrote to him regularly, complaining about things she did not like about the new house. Along with her complaints, she continued to express her worries about money matters. In his letters, Eastman assured her that they were wealthy enough to live in comfort and advised her to "get rid" of all her economical habits and "see how much money" she could "spend with good judgment."[22] Finally, to Eastman's frustration, his mother quit writing to him altogether. He had to resort to writing to friends to check on her.

London Factory

While in Europe, Eastman discovered that Walker had made no progress in establishing a new manufacturing plant in London. Walker claimed that his contract with Eastman did not include making financial deals and would have to be rewritten so he could be paid for the additional services. Eastman disagreed and Walker threatened to quit. Eastman suggested that Walker take a vacation and wait to leave the company until his replacement could be found. Eastman purchased a seven-acre site for the new factory in Harrow, right outside London. Then he spent a month meeting with architects, engineers, and contractors to get the factory started. Eastman worried about the delay and lost sales. He even complained that tourists were "in despair" and buying dry-plate cameras because Kodak cameras were not available.[23]

The problems between Eastman and Walker continued to escalate after Eastman returned home. Walker lacked confidence in the company's future. Halfway through the construction of the London factory, he expressed his concerns to Eastman. Annoyed, Eastman told him it was too late for him to be voicing his doubts about the project.[24]

Eastman tried to pacify his partner, but finally lost his patience. Once again, Walker submitted his resignation. This time, Eastman surprised him by accepting it. George Dickman was chosen to be Walker's replacement.

Conspiracy

On New Year's Day, 1892, Eastman became aware that four of his trusted employees, including Henry Reichenbach, were involved in a conspiracy. They planned to form a rival company and steal Eastman's emulsion formula and process. Eastman immediately fired the four men. Later, when he investigated the matter further, he discovered that Reichenbach had permitted 1,417 gallons of emulsion to spoil

Household Word

Kodak became a household word and other businesses tried to jump on the bandwagon. A candy maker produced Kodak bonbons. Alexander Black wrote a popular novel for young adults entitled *Captain Kodak: A Camera Story.* Webster Fulton wrote a popular song entitled "You Press the Button We Do the Rest" in which he alluded to the marvels of the Kodak camera. Fulton wrote:

Isn't it simple? Isn't it quick?

Such a small box. It must be a trick!

How do you work it? What is the test?

You press the button, we do the rest![25]

and allowed 39,400 feet of imperfect film to be sent to dealers. This resulted in a financial loss of nearly fifty thousand dollars. Eastman was bitterly disappointed. He had been fond of Reichenbach.[26]

Success

Even with the work of constant expansion and the recent conspiracy, Eastman's company continued to prosper. Within four years, thousands of people owned Kodak cameras and were taking their own snapshots. Due to his camera's success, Eastman changed the name of his company from Eastman Dry-Plate and Film Company to Eastman Kodak Company in May 1892. The following year his company "outstripped all competition and earned a profit of three million dollars."[27]

5

UPS AND DOWNS

In 1893, times were bad. The nation was in the middle of a depression. During the year, five hundred banks closed their doors, fifteen thousand businesses failed, railroads began to close, and mines were shut down. Unemployment soared in the cities. After three years, sales of Kodak cameras had peaked and begun sliding downward. In order to survive the storm, Eastman cut everyone's salary, including his own, by 25 percent. Due to Eastman's foresight and conservatism, his company ended 1893 with a net profit of $87,717—an outstanding feat during one of the worst economic years in American history.[1]

During this time, George Dickman managed to overcome the financial problems he inherited from his predecessor. Through his leadership, the English branch of the company started to pay its own way. He sent Eastman a two thousand dollar installment payment on a long-standing loan. "If I were subject to heart disease," Eastman wrote, "your cable might have been attended with fatal results."[2] He added that he could use the money.[3]

Search for New Emulsion-maker

After Reichenbach's defection, Eastman hired several emulsion-makers, but not one could make the grade. Emulsion-making was the most important part of manufacturing films—and the most unpredictable. Eastman joked he was going to call all his staff to a prayer meeting to pray for the emulsion.[4]

At a photographic convention, Eastman met William G. Stuber, from Louisville, Kentucky. Stuber was a nationally known portrait photographer and had spent six months in Switzerland studying emulsion-making techniques with a renowned scientist, Dr. John Henry Smith. Eastman was impressed with Stuber and offered him a job as foreman of his transparency plate department. The department produced glass dry plates that many professional photographers preferred to use instead of film.

Stuber accepted the position and began working at Kodak Park on January 4, 1894.

One day, Eastman asked Stuber why he thought Kodak film was good for only six months and then spoiled. Stuber replied he thought the problem had to do with the way the emulsion was made, not the ingredients. Eastman was surprised at his answer and instructed Stuber to test his theory.

Stuber conducted a few experiments and produced a batch of emulsion. After close comparison with current Kodak film, it was determined that Stuber's emulsion would last for years. Eastman had finally found a new emulsion-maker.

X rays

In 1895, Wilhelm C. Röntgen, a German scientist, discovered a new kind of invisible electromagnetic

X rays and the Human Body
The human body allows varying amounts of X-ray beams to pass through it. Soft tissues (blood, skin, fat, and muscle) permit almost all X rays to pass through them. They appear dark gray on film. Bone and tumor tissues are denser than soft tissues and allow a small amount of X rays to pass through them. They appear white on film. When a bone is broken, X-ray beams pass through the broken area and appear as a dark line on the white bone.

energy that could be used to produce images of internal tissues, bones, and organs on film. He called his discovery X rays because he did not understand what they were at first. The scientific symbol for the unknown is X.

One of Eastman's staff in Europe conveyed the news of Röntgen's discovery to him and sent him X-ray plates of a human hand and a frog. Eastman assigned William Stuber to look into the matter. A short time later, Kodak began manufacturing X-ray plates and developed small cardboard-backed film packets that could be used to make dental X rays.

Soule House

Eastman was unhappy with his rented house in Arnold Park. He wanted to own his own home with enough land surrounding it to build a stable and greenhouses. In August 1894, he became aware that the Soule House, one of the grandest houses in Rochester, was for sale. The two-year-old, three-story house was located at 400 East Avenue. The owner, Wilson Soule, died suddenly in an accident when he was caught in the reins of his own horse. Eastman bought the house from Soule's widow for one hundred thousand dollars, which included five hundred shares of Kodak stock.

Eastman told his mother that this time he was going to be in charge of the move.[5] He sent her to

New York City on a shopping trip with friends and asked his niece, Ellen Andrus, to come and help. It took three men with a horse-drawn wagon a day and a half to move Eastman's and his mother's belongings.

Eastman was not completely satisfied with the house. In a short time, he made fifteen thousand dollars worth of improvements. He had a window-less photography laboratory built in the basement, along with a shooting gallery. On the first floor, he installed an elaborate temperature control system with thermostats in five of the rooms. In his bed-room, he designed cubbyholes and drawers to store his personal possessions, ranging from his cuff links to silk hats. For his front yard, he purchased a ninety-foot flagpole and a twenty- by thirty-foot American flag. He also had plans drawn up for five greenhouses and hired the superintendent of Central Park in New York City, Samuel Parsons, to lay out the plants and flowers on the grounds around his house.

A Typical Day

At the turn of the twentieth century, George Eastman awoke each morning at 7:00 A.M. He dressed, selected a flower from his garden for his lapel, and went for a morning ride on his horse, Jaspar. After eating breakfast with his mother, he rode by carriage, bicycle, streetcar, or sleigh three miles into downtown Rochester to his office on State Street.

Often, he would come home for lunch and then visit the processing plants at Kodak Park before returning to his office. His mother was usually sitting in the bay window in the front of the house waiting for Eastman to return home after work. Servants later recalled that their boss "was never so animated as when he chronicled" his day's happenings to his mother.[6]

When not attending an evening social function, Eastman and his mother dined at home. One of his favorite pastimes after dinner was reading. Eastman subscribed to all five of Rochester's daily newspapers, several New York newspapers, the *London Times*, and numerous magazines. He also belonged to several book clubs and preferred to read nonfiction.

Philosophy of Life

Eastman was a practical man with a practical philosophy of life. Although he was the grandson of a Baptist minister, he did not attend church regularly. He adopted his personal philosophy of life from the writings of two ancient philosophers, Marcus Aurelius and Epictetus. They were called stoics and believed there was a divine plan for the universe and that everything happened for the best. Wealth and fame were not important to them. They were fatalists who "offered no hope for a personal immortality." In their teachings, they "counseled courage, an even temper and a sense of duty toward one's fellow men."[7] In their teachings, they promoted courage, a controlled temper, and selflessness. These were all ethical beliefs that Eastman embraced throughout his life.

World Market

"The manifest destiny of the Eastman Kodak Company," George Eastman wrote to his partner, Henry Strong, "is to be the largest manufacturer of photographic materials in the world, or else go to pot."[8] By 1896, Eastman had come a long way toward achieving his goal. That year, the one hundred thousandth Kodak camera was manufactured, and his company was producing film and photographic paper at the rate of three hundred to four hundred miles per month.

In order to meet the demand and continue to expand, more capital (funding) was needed. Without the assistance of financial brokers, Eastman refinanced and reorganized his company into one huge international corporation called Kodak Limited. He sold stock in his new company to investors in London for $12.5 million. By acting as his own financial broker and not paying bank fees,

Eastman made a personal profit of nearly a million dollars.

On the same day Kodak Limited was formed, George Dickman died. He had been ill for several weeks and died shortly after having abdominal surgery. In a letter to his mother, Eastman wrote that Dickman's death was a double loss. He had been both a capable business associate and a dear friend. Shortly before leaving Europe, he wrote to his mother again regarding Josephine, Dickman's widow: "I told her that when she felt like having a good rest that you would take her in and be a good mother to her."[9]

The "Divvy"

After returning from London, Eastman distributed $178,000 of his own money to his three thousand

Millionaires

When Eastman returned home to Rochester from Europe, he announced to his mother that they were now millionaires. She took his announcement in stride and replied, "That's nice, George."[10] She rarely talked about her son's money. Apparently, she felt he had made his fortune too late for her to enjoy it.

employees. He believed they deserved more than just good wages. He felt they should also be able to share in the profits his company made, just like stockholders.

Eastman referred to this bonus as the "divvy." An employee's divvy was based on his or her salary, the position he or she held in the company, and how long he or she had worked for Eastman. On one pay-day in early 1899, an extra paycheck was enclosed in each employee's pay envelope, along with a note:

> This is a personal matter with Mr. Eastman and he requests that you will not consider it as a gift, but as extra pay for extra good work.[11]

Suggestion Box

Another employee benefit Eastman established after returning from Europe was a monthly contest for employees to submit suggestions to improve operations. The notice posted regarding the new program stated that any suggestion, no matter how small, would be considered for an award. Every month, six cash prizes, ranging from $5 to $20, were awarded for the best suggestions. During the first year of the program, 579 suggestions were received, of which 332 received awards.

Patent Infringement

On September 12, 1898, Eastman became aware that patent examiners had reversed their decision and issued Reverend Hannibal Goodwin a patent for producing transparent film. Originally, Eastman had been given a patent because Goodwin's application had been too vague. Over a twelve-year period, Goodwin had revised his application several times and finally appealed to have his case reviewed on July 8, 1898. The patent examiners who reviewed the case found that the changes Goodwin had made in his application all stayed within his original specifications. This was an amazing turn of events. It opened the door for Goodwin to accuse Eastman of patent infringement.

Eastman answered Goodwin's charges in the *Kodak Trade Circular*, a trade publication:

> The facts of the matter are that Goodwin, after he had learned of our success in perfecting a process for the manufacture of rollable transparent films, and after we had successfully marketed such films, raked up an old application which he had sleeping in the Patent Office, copied into it a lot of matter he obtained from us . . . We do not think Goodwin ever had any workable process for making a transparent film . . . We have never heard of his using it.[12]

As far as Eastman was concerned, Goodwin would have to prove that he had a viable film product by producing it. He hired a private investigator to keep an eye on Goodwin. The investigator reported to Eastman that Goodwin had borrowed ten thousand dollars from a friend and was in the process of building a plant in Newark, New Jersey, to produce his film. Shortly afterward, Goodwin died from injuries after being hit by a streetcar. At the time, Eastman alerted his attorney that the Goodwin patent may soon be for sale and that he would be willing to pay a small amount to purchase it.

Brownie Camera

Concerning cameras, Eastman advised his staff that no single camera could "occupy every niche in the house of photography."[13] He constantly pushed them to create smaller, cheaper, and simpler models. The original Kodak camera was followed by No. 2 and No. 3 Kodaks, the ABC Kodaks, the Pocket Kodak, the Folding Kodak, and finally, the Brownie camera in 1900.

The Brownie cost one dollar and, according to Kodak advertising claims, anyone could take a good snapshot with a Brownie, even a child. In fact, advertising campaigns were geared toward children and the camera boxes were decorated with cartoon characters called "Brownies." Packaged along with the camera was a fifty-four-page instruction booklet and information on how to sign up for the Brownie Camera Club. The club charged no dues and members were eligible to participate in Kodak contests. Many professional photographers began their careers with a Brownie camera at an early age. The first batch of cameras sold out almost overnight.

Within a year, a quarter of a million people owned Brownie cameras.

A Family Wedding

On June 20, 1901, Eastman's niece, Ellen Andrus, married George Dryden of Cleveland. He had been a childhood friend of Ellen's and his background was similar to her uncle's. He, too, had dropped out of

Folding Kodak camera and a package of Kodak film

school to go to work at an early age. Dryden had started at the bottom in a company in the rubber business and climbed to the top until he owned his own company.

Eastman paid for the couple's elegant wedding. When the couple returned from their honeymoon, they stopped at Soule House and the two Georges went for a ride in a car together. When they returned, Eastman informed his niece that her husband did not talk very much. Ellen told her uncle that that was exactly what her husband had said about him. Instead of chatting, the two men had been sizing each other up. Later, Eastman decided that he liked Dryden. He told his niece that her husband was "all right."[14]

Business Practices

Eastman's success was based on his four basic business practices: mass production of goods at a low cost, international distribution of goods, extensive advertising of products, and customer service. These principles served him well during the many difficulties his company endured in the final decade of the nineteenth century.

This photograph of George Eastman was taken at the turn of the twentieth century.

6

MILLIONAIRE

Georgc Eastman had "a deep affection" for his hometown of Rochester.[1] He wanted to make it an attractive place to live and work for himself and his employees. Early in his career, he began to contribute financially to charitable local organizations and causes such as the Mechanics' Institute and Community War Chest.

University of Rochester

Eastman made his first major contribution to his community in 1902. Dr. Rush Rhees, the new president of the University of Rochester, asked Eastman to donate funds for a new biology and physics building. Rhees knew that Eastman's thriving photographic business was dependent on scientific research and thought Eastman might be interested in financing the building. Rhees estimated that the cost of the building would be fifty thousand dollars.

Rhees met with Eastman twice and found him to be "cordial and attentive."[2] He obtained a pledge from him for ten thousand dollars on the condition that the rest of the money to put up the new science building was obtained from other donors.

To Rhees's disappointment, he was able to raise only a small amount of money from former graduates and other friends of the university. He mustered up his courage and approached Eastman again. Eastman graciously increased his own pledge to sixty thousand dollars. When the construction of the building cost more than originally estimated, Eastman agreed to pick up the tab. He was given a master key to the building and he reluctantly allowed his name to be placed on the structure.

George Eastman House

In 1902, Eastman was finally able to purchase farmland in Rochester to build his dream home. He bought what he called the last farm within the city limits of Rochester.[3] The eight-and-a-half-acre piece of property was located on East Avenue just down the street from the Soule House. Within a few months, he hired an architect to design a colonial revival-style mansion and a landscape architect to lay out the grounds.[4] He wanted to be able "to raise animals, grow vegetables, and entertain guests" in beautiful surroundings.[5]

The stately fifty-room, four-story, stone-columned mansion took three years to build and cost five hundred thousand dollars (around $5 million today). The house had its own electric generator, a twenty-one-station internal phone system, a built-in vacuum cleaning system, an elevator, and a central clock network. Eastman mandated that the house be as fireproof as possible. He had spent many years working around highly flammable chemicals and wanted to make sure his home could not be destroyed by fire. Because of this, the house was built of steel-reinforced concrete. The outer walls were fourteen inches thick. In addition, solid steel sliding doors were installed in the walls beside doorways so they could be pulled closed to isolate a fire.

Located on the main floor of the house were a living room, small library, billiard room, music conservatory, and dining room. In the conservatory, Eastman installed an organ, which cost $30,319.25. It was considered the top of the line in organs.[6] Upstairs were fifteen bedrooms, each with its own bathroom. On the third floor, Eastman had a laboratory where he cooked and experimented with photography; a projector room to show home movies; and a storeroom for his guns, fishing tackle, and camping gear. Eastman was an avid hunter and owned a hunting lodge in North Carolina.

The grounds surrounding the house were extensive. They included a lily pond, flower gardens, vegetable gardens, a rock garden, orchards, berry patches, greenhouses, stables, a tool house and repair shop, a carriage house, and barns. Eastman was fond of his animals and gave each one a name.

The George Eastman House is located at 900 East Avenue in Rochester, New York.

Twenty-eight servants, who were supervised by a professional housekeeper, staffed Eastman's home. The housekeeper had a yearly operating budget of one hundred thousand dollars. At Eastman's request, she compiled monthly reports containing information on the milk yielded by his five Jersey cows, how much butter was churned from cream obtained from the cow's milk, how many eggs were laid by his chickens, and how many peaches were grown in his orchard.

House Warming

On October 7, 1905, Eastman entertained for the first time in his new home. Because his mother had broken her hip and was unable to serve as his hostess, Eastman invited only men to the affair. One hundred of Kodak's top officials attended. They dined on a nine-course meal while a male quartet and organist performed. After dinner, a vaudeville act entertained the group, followed by fireworks. The evening ended with everyone singing *Auld Lang Syne*.

Mother's Death

Confined to a wheelchair since falling and breaking her hip, Maria Eastman became bedridden in the spring of 1907. She developed bronchitis and died on June 16. She was eighty-five years old. When his

Maria Eastman, sitting in a wheelchair, poses with her two great-grandchildren.

mother died, Eastman said he cried "all day" and "could not have stopped to save my life."[7]

Maria Eastman's funeral was held at St. Paul's Episcopal Church in downtown Rochester. Reverend Murray Bartlett officiated at the services. Numerous floral tributes were sent by Kodak employees. Kodak offices opened two hours later than usual that morning. Following the service a funeral train took Eastman and his family to Waterville, New York, where Maria was buried next to her husband and daughter Katy.

When she died, Maria Eastman's estate was valued at $102,856.31. She left $4,350 to seventeen servants, $17,500 to eighteen relatives, and the remaining $81,000 to her son. Eastman gave his niece, Ellen Dryden, $40,000, and wrote and told her that he was also putting $40,000 in bonds in a safe-deposit box for her brother Royal. Eastman felt his twenty-nine-year-old nephew was careless with his money. He wanted to wait until Royal was more responsible before he got his share of his grandmother's estate.

Josephine Dickman

After his mother's death, Eastman's friendship with Josephine Dickman blossomed. They had many common interests: music, art, travel, and photography. He showered her with gifts such as butter churns, cows, music lessons, handkerchiefs, and a picnic set of his own design. She also helped him hire household staff. They often traveled together and photographed each other. In 1908, they went on a fishing trip to Wyoming. One night while sitting beside the campfire, Josephine began to sing. When coyotes started to accompany her, Eastman almost doubled over laughing.

Goodwin Lawsuit

Before Eastman's attorney could negotiate a deal with Goodwin's widow, the Anthony Company purchased Goodwin's film patent from her. Shortly afterward, the owners of the Anthony Company offered to sell Eastman the film patent for a million dollars. They implied that if Eastman did not purchase it from them, they would sue him for patent infringement. Eastman disliked being threatened. He balked at the idea of paying a million dollars for the patent for film that had never been manufactured.

After Eastman's refusal, the Anthony Company began producing film using the Goodwin process. They called their new product Ansco film. Within a week of producing their first roll, they made good on their threat. They filed a lawsuit against Eastman Kodak for patent infringement. After filing the lawsuit, the owners of the Anthony Company offered to sell their business and the Goodwin patent to

Eastman. They told him that if he bought their company, he would have a monopoly and could raise prices. Eastman declined their offer. He indignantly informed them that his goal was "to lower prices not to raise them."[8]

Antitrust Suit

The legal battle over the Goodwin patent had been going on for several years when Eastman was challenged by another lawsuit. In October 1911, he was informed that the U.S. Attorney General's office was investigating his company for possible violation of the Sherman Antitrust Act. The antitrust law was passed in 1890 due to the public outcry against big businesses that were buying out their competitors and forming monopolies. By eliminating their competition, these companies were able to raise prices and make outrageous profits. The law, designed to protect free competition, prohibited any contract, combination, or conspiracy to restrain trade.

Eastman Kodak controlled 90 percent of the photographic supply business in the United States and was well on its way to dominating the world market as well.[9] Many of Kodak's competitors were jealous of the company's dominant position in the industry. They were determined to prove that Kodak was violating antitrust laws. The government investigated Eastman's business practices for nearly two years and then began formal antitrust proceedings against his company.

Wage Dividends

Even though he was involved in a lawsuit, Eastman decided to give his employees a wage dividend. Dividends are the share of a company's profits that are usually paid to stockholders. Eastman felt his employees were just as entitled to dividends as the stockholders who had invested in his company.

Beginning on July 1, 1912, all of Eastman's 5,179 worldwide employees received a 2 percent wage dividend based on their wages over the past five years.[10] "You can talk about cooperation and good feelings and friendliness from morning to midnight,"

Premature Obituary

In April 1912, George Eastman had the morbid experience of reading his own obituary in a newspaper. According to the article, he had perished aboard the *Titanic* when it struck an iceberg and sank over two hours later. The new ocean liner was on its maiden voyage from Southampton, England, to New York City. Over fifteen hundred people died in the disaster, including millionaire John Jacob Astor. It is possible that George Eastman had been confused with Astor.

he told *The New York Times*, "but the thing the worker appreciates is the same thing the man at the helm appreciates—dollars and cents."[11]

Goodwin Lawsuit Settled

On August 8, 1913, the court finally handed down its ruling concerning the Goodwin patent case. Eastman Kodak lost. Eastman's attorneys appealed, but advised Eastman to settle the case out of court. Since the decision covered "all Kodak film ever made," the situation was dangerous.[12] If the appeal failed, the Eastman Kodak Company might not be able to survive.

Eastman began negotiating with a representative of the Anthony Company. He was told that they were willing to settle out of court for $6 million. Eastman countered with $3.5 million. His offer was refused. Then he offered $5 million in cash, which was accepted. The amount of the settlement was not made public. Eastman paid the $5 million out of his own pocket, possibly because he did not want Kodak stockholders to know how close the company had come to total disaster.

After the ruling in the Goodwin lawsuit, Eastman was apprehensive about losing the antitrust suit against him, too. In a letter to Dr. Rush Rhees, Eastman wrote about his feelings concerning the case. He felt that the government's position appeared to be that, if a company had been "built up in violation of the law," it was not enough for the company "to reform your evil practices" but they must "be dissolved" and if they cannot be dissolved then they "must be destroyed."[13] Eastman had no choice but to wait patiently and see what would happen.

$\boxed{7}$

PHILANTHROPIST

George Eastman felt that if a man was wealthy, he had a choice to make. His money was piling up. He could either let it accumulate and leave it to "others to administer when he is dead" or he could "get it into action and have fun, while he is still alive."[1] Even though the antitrust lawsuit was still hanging over his head, Eastman opted to get "into action" and start "adapting" his money "to human needs, and making the plan work."[2]

African-American Education

One of the first charities outside of Rochester that Eastman supported was African-American education. He developed an interest in African Americans and their education after reading Booker T. Washington's autobiography, *Up from Slavery*. Eastman was impressed with the practical way Washington had overcome his difficult background.

Washington, who had been born a slave, worked as a manual laborer after the Civil War. He was mostly self-taught until he attended the Hampton Normal and Agricultural Institute. At Hampton, he learned to be a brick mason but was such a good speaker that he started teaching. At the age of twenty-five, he was appointed principal of the newly established Tuskegee Institute.

Washington advocated that his students try to better themselves through vocational training, economic self-reliance, and efficiency in their work. Eastman endorsed all three of these principles for everyone, not just African Americans. He requested copies of Tuskegee's annual report and periodically sent the institute funds to use for whatever it needed. He also occasionally donated funds to the Hampton Institute, where Washington had been educated.

In 1914, Eastman gave Tuskegee five thousand dollars to build a veterinary hospital. The building was dedicated in May 1915. Washington sent Eastman a photograph of the dedication ceremony. Five months later, after studying Tuskegee's current annual report, Eastman wrote Washington and

Booker T. Washington was grateful for George Eastman's generosity.

informed him that he would donate two hundred fifty thousand dollars to the school's building fund, if the school would raise enough money to pay off all its debts.

Unfortunately, Washington died six days later. Eastman immediately wrote to the institute and informed its officers that his offer was still good. He had been thinking about it for a long time. He felt it was important that Tuskegee's friends continue to support the school and not allow the school to lose ground due to the sudden loss of Washington.

The Massachusetts Institute of Technology

Another educational institution that impressed Eastman was the Massachusetts Institute of Technology (MIT). Over the years, MIT had supplied Eastman with several key employees, and he had a great deal of confidence in the school's graduates' abilities. For nearly two decades, Eastman scrutinized MIT's annual reports. When Richard C. Maclaurin became president of the institute in 1909, Eastman made it known that he wanted to meet him.

Maclaurin seized the opportunity and approached Eastman about donating funds to develop a new campus for the institute. The school had purchased a fifty-acre site along the Charles River in eastern Massachusetts with the assistance of another philanthropist, but had no funds to build on the site. Eastman agreed to donate $2.5 million to the school's building fund, provided he received no public recognition for the gift. He specified that his name had to be withheld. Maclaurin agreed to Eastman's terms, and when he announced the largest donation the institute had ever received to his executive committee, he called the donor "Mr. Smith, just Mr. Smith."[3]

Eastman enjoyed the public guessing game that followed the announcement of his donation. No one suspected that the sixty-two-year-old photography millionaire was Mr. Smith. Eastman was unknown nationally as a philanthropist and that was the way he liked it. He was a shy man and did not like to call attention to himself.

Antitrust Suit Continues

The court hearings in the antitrust lawsuit against Eastman Kodak alternated between Buffalo and Rochester, New York. Federal Judge John R. Hazel, who had presided over the Goodwin lawsuit, also presided over these hearings. During the trial, Eastman defended his business practices. He felt that selling high-quality goods at a fair, fixed price served the public better than manufacturing wars in which prices were slashed and products cheapened. He did not try to hide the fact that his company had bought out numerous competitors in order to provide "a complete line of the very best photographic materials and apparatus. . . ."[4]

Judge Hazel was not convinced by Eastman's arguments. On August 24, 1915, he ruled that Eastman Kodak Company had created a monopoly "in the trade of photographic goods by signing exclusive contracts with the leading European paper manufacturers, by purchasing competing businesses, and by imposition of fixed prices on its goods."[5] The judge decreed that, in order to satisfy the intent of the law, the Eastman Kodak Company would have to be divided into two or more competing companies. The judge, however, did not stipulate how this division should take place. To buy time, Eastman's lawyers appealed Judge Hazel's decision to the U.S. Supreme Court.

Loss of a Friend

In the fall of 1916, while Eastman was preparing to go to his hunting lodge in North Carolina for Thanksgiving, he received word that Josephine Dickman had died. While staying at the Copley Plaza Hotel, she had passed away in her sleep. Eastman left immediately for the funeral in Boston. Train connections were difficult and Eastman arrived forty-five minutes late. Josephine's friends had the organist play, stalling the start of the service, until Eastman arrived.

Several months later, the executor of Josephine Dickman's estate inquired whether there were any of her personal effects that Eastman would like to have. Eastman chose the picnic set he had sent her. His most pleasant memories of Josephine Dickman were associated with their camping and picnicking together.

Mr. Smith

Eastman increased his donation to MIT before construction of the new campus was completed. He added another $500,000, making his total donation to the building fund $3 million. At the time, he also gave $300,000 to the chemistry department to help educate chemical engineers on how to effectively handle industrial problems. Eastman cleverly allowed MIT to identify him as the donor of the funding for the chemistry department. This kept people from guessing the identity of Mr. Smith.

When the new MIT campus opened in 1916, banquets were held simultaneously in thirty-six cities to celebrate MIT's success. Because of Eastman's donation to the chemistry department, he attended the banquet that was held in Rochester. The celebrations were linked by telephone, and when Mr. Smith's latest donation was announced, Eastman cheered as loudly as the rest of the audience. He appeared to thoroughly enjoy the deception and it was several years before he was identified as "Mr. Smith."

World War I

The final resolution of the antitrust lawsuit was interrupted by a war in Europe. The war broke out when Archduke Franz Ferdinand, the crown prince of Austria-Hungary, was killed by an assassin. The assassin, Gavrilo Princip, was a member of a Serbian terrorist organization called the Black Hand. Princip believed that the Serbian people had the right to govern themselves and resented his people being dominated by Austria-Hungary.

Many people believed that the Serbian government had actually ordered Franz Ferdinand's murder. Austria-Hungary declared war on Serbia, and within a few weeks, the main powers of Europe took sides in the conflict. Germany backed Austria-Hungary. France, Great Britain, and Russia sided with Serbia.

As the guns of war rumbled through Europe, George Eastman quickly left for England to check on his overseas operation. All communications with his branch offices, except for the Paris, France, office, had been shut down. There was nothing he could do. He returned home resolved to wean his company from its dependence on European raw materials as soon as possible.

At first, Eastman tried to remain neutral and not take sides in the conflict. When the Germans invaded Belgium and then sank the *Lusitania* with three people from Rochester aboard, Eastman changed his mind. He decided it was time for the United States to become involved in the conflict.

When the United States did declare war on Germany on March 17, 1917, Eastman plunged into the war effort. He became chairman of the Rochester Red Cross, a national organization that worked to relieve human suffering in wartime. He vigorously raised funds to buy war bonds to support the war. During the war, the United States government borrowed money from citizens by selling them war bonds. Later, the war bonds were paid back with interest. Also, Eastman offered to supply the government with cellulose acetate, a chemical compound that could be used to waterproof airplane wings, and to set up a school for aerial photography at Kodak Park. Aerial photographs could be used to determine enemy operations during the war. The government accepted Eastman's offer to provide chemicals to waterproof airplane wings. They passed, however, on his offer to establish an aerial photography school. "It may be that the government is afraid to accept any favors from one of the so-called trusts," Eastman commented. "Of course we are not paying any attention to such discrimination, but are trying to help out wherever we can."[6]

"Whistling Jim"

Even though the government declined Eastman's offer to establish an aerial photography school, they were interested in his company's developing an aerial mapping camera. Eastman's staff went to work on the project and developed an automatic aerial camera that they nicknamed "Whistling Jim." The camera was loaded with fifty-foot rolls of film and could be operated at the same time a soldier was manning a machine gun mounted in an airplane. Eastman's staff also designed a gun sight for machine guns that increased the ability of machine gunners to accurately hit a target during dogfights.[7]

Home Front

On the home front, Eastman had his lawns plowed up and planted with potatoes and onions. In a time when many foods were in short supply, he felt that his gardeners could be put to better use growing food than cutting grass. His household also conserved sugar and observed certain meatless and wheatless days, even though he was certainly wealthy enough to ignore such wartime rules.

Aerial School of Photography

In January 1918, the U.S. War Department had a change of heart. It decided to take Eastman up on his offer to establish a school for aerial photography.

Within two months, the first class of two hundred fifty men arrived in Rochester to begin training. The fourth floor of a new paper mill at Kodak Park was turned into classrooms and a barracks to house the soldiers. They ate their meals in the Kodak Park cafeteria, and their instructors were Kodak employees. They learned the basics of aerial photography, including camera operation and repair, film processing, and interpretation of reconnaissance photographs. Before the war ended, nearly two thousand men graduated from the school.

A truce was declared at the end of November 1918. Eight months later, World War 1 officially ended when the Treaty of Versailles was signed on June 28, 1919. Shortly after the war ended, Eastman had his accountants review his company's war contracts with the federal government. He had no intention of making a profit from the war and refunded $182,770 back to the government. When he was informed of Eastman's actions, President Warren Harding wrote to Eastman to thank him for his "very prompt and considerate action on the part of your company in making a wholly voluntary adjustment after the close of a great war service."[8]

Antitrust Suit Settled

By the end of the war, the government's attitude toward large corporations had softened. Possibly,

Eastman Kodak's involvement in the war effort had helped. In 1921, George Eastman was finally able to settle the antitrust case against him by agreeing to sell certain factories and equipment. Fortunately, the factories he agreed to part with made up only a fraction of his business. Plus, they were producing goods that would soon be obsolete, such as dry plates, plate cameras, and certain types of paper. Eastman wrote to William Gifford, one of his former attorneys, that he did not want to brag, but "the settlement is a favorable one."[9] The Eastman Kodak Company would not be greatly damaged.

8

MEDICINE
AND MUSIC

Of all the charitable projects Eastman undertook, his favorite and the one he felt gave him the most return for his money was the dental clinics he established for children. "Dollar for dollar," Eastman told Cyrus Curtis of the *Saturday Evening Post*, "I got more from my investment in the Rochester Dental Dispensary [clinic] than from anything else to which I contributed."[1]

Eastman's interest in dental care arose from his family's own experiences. Eastman's mother had suffered devastating toothaches and had to have fifteen of her teeth pulled. At the time, few so-called dentists had any medical training. They used pliers

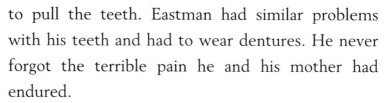

Children

Although George Eastman had no children of his own, he enjoyed their company. When friends visited with their children, he acted like a kindly grandfather, stopping to tie a shoe or requesting that his butler cut up a young visitor's meat.

One of his favorite stories was about his chauffeur's daughter. She lived with her family in a house on the University Avenue side of Eastman's home. She often played in Eastman's garden and would chat with him when he was outside. One day, someone asked her if she knew Mr. Eastman. "Oh yes," she replied. "I know him well. He lives in my backyard."[2]

to pull the teeth. Eastman had similar problems with his teeth and had to wear dentures. He never forgot the terrible pain he and his mother had endured.

His desire for local children to be provided dental care in their formative years led Eastman to build the Alexander Street Clinic in Rochester in 1917. Eastman paid $402,972.88 for the construction of a functional U-shaped building to house the clinic. Children up to the age of sixteen were to be provided dental care at the clinic for the minimal fee of five cents per visit. If a family earned less than five dollars a week, its children could get care at the clinic until they were twenty-one years old. The clinic became a model for more than half a dozen clinics Eastman later established in London, Paris, Rome, Brussels, and Stockholm. In all five European cities, Eastman Kodak had branch offices or manufacturing facilities.

Music

George Eastman loved music and made it an integral part of his life. In 1919, he hired Harold Gleason as his personal organist. Gleason played for Eastman every morning for an hour while he ate breakfast. He was also required to provide music every Wednesday evening for Eastman and his guests after dinner and to accompany other musicians entertaining at Eastman's home on Sunday evenings. Gleason later commented that as far as he knew, Eastman "was the first and last person in the United States to maintain such an elaborate musical establishment in his home."[3]

Eastman made no pretense about the fact that he was not a musician himself. In fact, he admitted he was practically "a musical moron" because he could not carry a tune or even remember a tune.[4] Nevertheless, he loved to listen to music and he wanted to share this joy with others and make music a part of their lives.

When the director of music for the Rochester public schools informed Eastman that his department

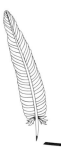

Music Conservatory

After fourteen years, Eastman decided that his music conservatory was too small for the concerts, plays, and other entertaining he liked to hold in his home. He consulted an architectural firm about his plan to enlarge his house by cutting it in half and rolling one part away from the other.

The architects tried to discourage him, but Eastman was determined. He hired a Pittsburgh construction company, which cut his house in two and rolled one section nine feet away from the other on logs and railroad ties. The resulting gap was enclosed with new walls. Eastman avidly photographed the project and was proud of the fact that as a layman, he had come up with an architecturally sound plan to expand his house.

had plenty of music teachers but needed more band and orchestra instruments, Eastman donated fifteen thousand dollars to the department. The funds were used to purchase two hundred fifty musical instruments. A program was also set up for students to borrow instruments at no cost for a year or longer.

Medical Center

In the spring of 1920, Eastman was approached by Abraham Flexner, a recognized authority on higher education, about the possibility of establishing a School of Medicine in Rochester. Flexner had written a controversial report concerning the weaknesses of medical education in the United States. At the time, physicians went through apprenticelike training, working with other physicians. Flexner felt there was a need for scientifically-based medical teaching programs in which instructors devoted themselves exclusively to teaching and research.

Due to his report, Flexner was hired by John D. Rockefeller, Sr., to be the administrator of his General Education Board. Rockefeller put Flexner in charge of spending $100 million from his vast fortune on improving medical education in the United States.

Flexner approached Dr. Rush Rhees about adding a school of medicine to the University of Rochester. Rhees felt that providing medical education was a costly endeavor. Once again, he was not interested unless sufficient funding could be found

John D. Rockefeller

The son of a poor peddler, John D. Rockefeller made his fortune in the petroleum (oil) industry. In 1870, he established the Standard Oil Company and became one of the wealthiest men in the United States. In 1897, he retired and began giving his vast fortune away. During his lifetime, he donated $520 million to charitable causes.

to create a first-class school. Even though he was not fully behind the idea, Rhees arranged for Flexner to meet with George Eastman.

Eastman spent nearly a whole day talking with Flexner. He was definitely interested in the project but had already pledged a great deal of his money to other projects. After Flexner left Rochester, Eastman thought about the project for several weeks. Finally, he decided to donate $5 million if Rockefeller would match his donation. Eastman also wanted the dental clinic he had established earlier to become part of the medical school.

The University of Rochester's School of Medicine and Dentistry was started in 1920. The agreement between Eastman and Rockefeller made headlines across the country.

Tonsil Clinic

During dental visits, children were also examined for nose, throat, and mouth defects. A large number of the children were noted to have diseased adenoids and tonsils. (Tonsils are a mass of specialized tissue found on each side of the back of the throat. Adenoids are glandlike tissues in the upper throat, behind the nasal passage.) At the time, doctors believed diseased tonsils made children more susceptible to infectious diseases. Eastman decided, with the backing of the medical community, that it

In this photograph, a dentist checks the mouth of a young patient in a North Carolina clinic in 1921.

would be a good idea "to remove every tonsil from every schoolchild in Rochester" and he wanted it done immediately.[5] He provided the money, organized the clinics, and persuaded school authorities and hospital staff to work together. In the tonsillectomy marathon that resulted from his efforts, more than seven thousand sets of tonsils were removed. Today, doctors are not as likely to perform tonsillectomies. They now believe tonsils help the body fight infection.

School of Music

One day, unexpectedly, Eastman asked Dr. Rush Rhees if he would like to see a school of music at the University of Rochester. Rhees supported the idea. Shortly after discussing the school with Rhees, Eastman purchased the property, equipment, and corporate rights to the Institute of Musical Art in Rochester and turned the organization over to the university. Then, he purchased property on the southeast corner of Gibbs and Main Streets in Rochester to build a small concert hall and movie theater. Eastman planned for musical concerts to be given one day a week in the concert hall and for motion pictures to be shown six days a week in the theater, accompanied by orchestra music. At the time, motion pictures were silent and normally accompanied by live music.

Eastman expected the proceeds from the movie theater to help support the school's orchestra. He also expected his "great music project" to influence moviegoers and give them an appreciation for quality music.[6] His theory was that people who had little interest in music would gradually grow to appreciate it when they heard it "day after day." They would realize "the place it ought to occupy in their lives."[7] The school was formally dedicated on March 3, 1922. Unfortunately, the movie theater operated at a loss. Eventually, Eastman closed it down.

LATER YEARS

After World War I, George Eastman continued to be preoccupied with putting his money to good use in his lifetime. He had donated over $45 million to various organizations, but he was still not satisfied. On December 8, 1924, after a formal dinner party at his home, Eastman remarked that "Men who leave their money to be distributed by others are pie-faced mutts."[1] Then he picked up a pen and signed a document giving away $30 million. Eastman's donation was divided among MIT, the Hampton Institute, the Tuskegee Institute, and the University of Rochester. Witnessing the event were ten men representing the four educational institutions. After signing the document, Eastman smiled and remarked, " . . . now I feel better."[2]

Retirement

When Eastman reached the age of sixty-nine, he began to withdraw from the active management of Eastman Kodak Company. In a letter to a friend, he wrote that what he wanted to do was fade away and retire quietly. He felt there was "a lot of young blood in the Company," and he wanted to organize it so that people could say after he was gone that "the old man was not the whole thing after all."[3]

Calendar Reform

In his semiretirement, Eastman adopted a new cause: calendar reform. A friend in New York City sent Moses B. Cotsworth, a British statistician, to Rochester to meet with Eastman. Cotsworth had spent twenty-five years promoting the adoption of a thirteen-month calendar. He had exhausted his personal financial resources and was looking for someone to help him continue his campaign.

Cotsworth felt that the main problem with the Gregorian calendar used today was that months were not exact multiples of weeks. Some months had four weeks and others five. He proposed a simple calendar based on thirteen months, each consisting of twenty-eight days, for a total of 364 days in a year. Since there are 365 days in a year, he suggested that the extra day be a worldwide holiday called World Peace Day. He also suggested that the thirteenth month be called Sol and that it be placed on the calendar between the months of June and July. Cotsworth also advocated that Easter be assigned a specific date and all holidays be held on Mondays.

Cotsworth's useful plan appealed to Eastman. However, before supporting his cause financially, Eastman wanted to see how realistic it would be to expect people to make such a big change in their lives. His staff put together an attractive booklet entitled "Do We Need Calendar Reform?" and composed a questionnaire that was sent to one hundred people from various occupations, along with a personal letter from Eastman. When a large percentage of the questionnaires returned with favorable responses, Eastman decided to help Cotsworth.

A number of large businesses adopted the thirteen-month calendar plan, including Eastman Kodak Company. The League of Nations supported the plan and numerous church organizations liked the idea of Easter being celebrated on a specific date each year. Unfortunately, due to people's resistance to change, the only part of Cotsworth's plan that was adopted in the United States was the observance of nonreligious holidays on Mondays.

Saturday Lunches

In his later years, Eastman invited a group of four young married women to his home regularly for Saturday lunches. The group consisted of Mrs. George Whipple, wife of the dean of the medical school; Mrs. Harold Gleason, wife of Eastman's organist; Mrs. Stanhope Bayne-Jones, wife of a professor of bacteriology at the University of Rochester; and Mrs. Marion Folsom, wife of an Eastman Kodak executive. They were like nieces to Eastman. "He was comfortable with us," Mrs. Whipple once said.

Young Barbara Whipple says good-bye to George Eastman.

"He could even doze off after lunch and know that we would go on talking among ourselves."[4]

The group often dined on lobster shipped in from Boston and talked about cooking, plumbing, bringing up babies, politics, and women's fashions. Eastman subscribed to *Vogue* magazine and kept up with the latest fashions. He was rather opinionated about the colors women wore. He disliked black and liked to see women in bright colors.[5]

Africa Safari

Eastman officially retired from Eastman Kodak in 1925. The following year, he packed his bags and set out for Africa. He was over seventy years old, and his family and friends warned him that Africa, often called the Dark Continent, was full of many dangers. Their concern made Eastman even more determined to go. Eastman had always enjoyed hunting and felt it might be his last chance to go big game hunting.

For his traveling companions Eastman chose Dr. Audley Stewart, his personal physician, and Daniel Pomeroy, a friend and banker. Carl Akeley, a naturalist and explorer, would join the group in Africa with a work crew from the American Museum of Natural History in New York. The hunters had agreed to supply specimens for an African Hall exhibit the museum planned to build.

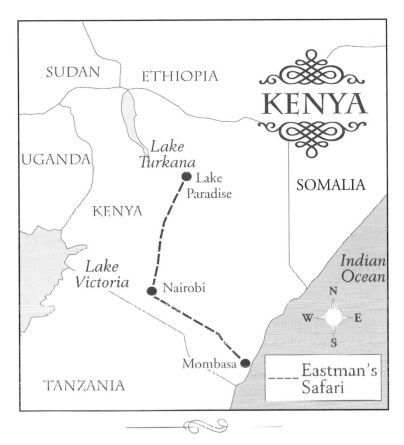

This map shows the route that George Eastman took on his safari through Kenya in 1926.

Eastman, accompanied by Stewart and Pomeroy, left Rochester for Europe on March 13, 1926. They spent a few weeks in London and Paris and then sailed to Africa. From Mombasa, a seaport on the southeastern coast of Kenya, they traveled by train to Nairobi, where Osa and Martin Johnson met them. The Johnsons were wildlife photographers. They had established a campsite, called Lake Paradise, in Kedong Valley, where they observed and filmed animal life. Eastman, along with several other backers, had supported the Johnsons' endeavors for several years.

Anticipating Eastman's arrival, the Johnsons built a special log cabin for him at Lake Paradise. The cabin had a veranda and was built alongside an elephant trail. Several times a day, the large animals passed by, giving Eastman an opportunity to photograph them.

Snakes for Dinner

On the second night at Lake Paradise, while the group was eating dinner, Osa noticed that Eastman's water glass was empty. She was about to ask one of her staff to fill Eastman's glass when she noticed a cobra crawling toward Eastman's foot. She signaled someone to do something about the snake. A servant killed it quickly with a club. "A fine Hostess you are," Eastman jokingly said to Osa. "Snakes for dinner."[6]

Eastman was impressed with Osa's ability to create a homey environment in the wilderness. He treated her like an adopted daughter and never seemed to get over her "pink-silk-dress-little-girlness," as he called it, in contrast to her "ruggedness on safari."[7]

Often Eastman assisted Osa and her staff in cooking meals. He prepared muffins, cornbread, biscuits, or other items from his own recipes on the

Eastman's Lemon Pie Recipe

6 eggs

2 lemons

I cup sugar

Beat the yolks of six eggs with one cup of granulated sugar. Add grated rind and juice of two lemons. Cook fifteen minutes in double boiler, stirring constantly. Take from fire, and when cool, add the beaten whites of three eggs. Fill a pie crust that has been baked a light brown. Make meringue with three remaining egg whites, top off, and put in oven to brown.[8]

camp stove. One of his favorite items to cook was lemon pie. He never seemed to get enough of it and always ate at least two large slices.

Rhino Incident

One day while hunting, the group came across an old rhinoceros. Eastman was fascinated by the animal. He took out his home movie camera and began walking toward the animal until he was only twenty yards away from it. Later, Osa Johnson wrote:

> Suddenly the big beast . . . snorted, and lowered his head and charged. Never have I seen a greater exhibition of coolness than Mr. Eastman displayed. Instead of turning and running, which anyone else would have done, he stood quietly, still facing the animal and then when . . . it was within perhaps fifteen feet of him, he simply side-stepped it, like a toreador [bull fighter] and actually touched its side as it passed.[9]

George Eastman stands in his garden with his Kodak movie camera.

Several months later, when Eastman returned to Rochester, he was entertaining a distinguished group of surgeons and showed them the movie he had made from his African safari. After the rhino incident, the group scolded Eastman and told him he should have been more careful. When their protests subsided, Eastman quietly remarked, "Well, you've got to trust your organization."[10] Obviously, Eastman had a high regard for the people who worked for him and felt that a leader needed to trust his employees.

Back to Africa

Although his health was questionable and he seemed to be suffering constantly from colds—Eastman returned to Africa with the Johnsons in January 1928. This time, they went to Egypt and sailed down the Nile River. Then Eastman proceeded by car to Uganda in the Belgian Congo where elephants and white rhinoceroses could be hunted.

On February 2, Eastman shot a white rhinoceros and an elephant. Eastman wanted to display the elephant's head on the wall in his home, but when the dead elephant was turned over, it was discovered he had only one tusk. Eastman, who had worn false teeth for years, was not disappointed. He remarked, "we'll have a false one made for him."[11] When Eastman said good-bye to the Johnsons at the end of

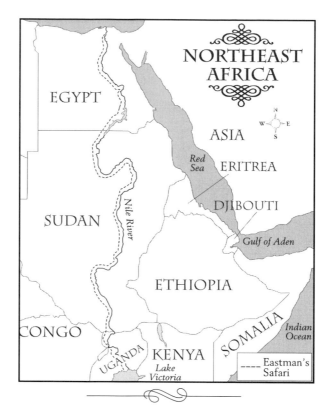

This map of present-day Africa shows the route George Eastman took on his safari through northeast Africa in 1928.

his second safari, he told them, "This had been the happiest period of my entire life."[12]

Loss of Vigor

After returning from his second trip to Africa, Eastman began to slow down. He was still suffering from frequent colds, and he started napping in the middle of the day, something he had never done before. Eastman was seventy-five years old and his physician could not find anything specifically wrong.[13]

Kodak's Fiftieth Anniversary

To commemorate the fiftieth anniversary of the Eastman Kodak Company, five hundred thousand specially designed Kodak cameras were given away to children who were celebrating their twelfth birthday in 1930. The cameras and a free roll of Kodak film were to be distributed by Kodak dealers during the entire month of May 1930; however, within three days, all the cameras were gone.

In advertisements promoting the camera giveaway, Eastman's company expressed its appreciation to parents and grandparents who "played so important a part in development of amateur picture-taking in America. . . ." According to the advertisements, the reason for the giveaway was to "raise amateur photography, among the coming generation, to even greater heights . . . For, as amateur photography increases in popularity, the use of Kodak products will increase with it."[14]

In 1929, Eastman said he did not feel ill, "just good for nothing."[15] He stayed home most of the time, going outside only for occasional rides. He passed the time reading murder mysteries. Always dressed in a business suit and shoes, never house slippers, he would sit in a leather chair in front of the fireplace in his sitting room, reading.

In 1930, Eastman began to experience a great deal of pain in his back and legs. When he walked, he dragged one of his feet behind him. Finally, Eastman's physician determined that he had spinal stenosis, the hardening of the cells in the lower part of his spinal cord. Eastman asked his physician what course the disease would take. He was told that it was progressive and irreversible. Eastman knew he would soon be an invalid confined to a wheelchair or

On July 28, 1928, the announcement of Eastman's Kodacolor home-movie system was celebrated at the George Eastman House. Pictured are (from left to right) Lewis Perry, George Eastman, Charles Lindbergh, Thomas Edison, Henry Ford, and Samuel Wesley Stratton.

George Eastman was an avid reader. In this photograph, he is reading in the sitting room of the George Eastman House.

his bed. He dreaded the thought of becoming dependent on others.

New Will

The fact that he still had $8 million in cash in the bank and owned millions of dollars' worth of stocks and bonds concerned Eastman. Since he intended to leave only a small inheritance to his niece, Ellen Dryden, and her children, he decided it was time to change his will.

Eastman asked Milton Robinson, a Kodak attorney, to draw up a new will. He wanted to leave his remaining fortune to the University of Rochester. He also designated his house to be used as the official residence of the president of the university and established a $2 million endowment to maintain it.

On Monday, March 14, 1932, several old friends arrived at Eastman's home to witness the signing of his new will. Eastman was in a good mood and even insisted on placing the chairs in his room for his guests by himself.

When the fountain pen Eastman was using refused to work, Frank Crouch, Eastman's former office manager, commented that he could certainly afford to buy a new pen. Eastman told Crouch not to complain about his pen because Crouch had given it to him. As his friends were leaving the room, Eastman asked his secretary to give each of them a twenty-dollar gold piece.

Shortly after Eastman was left alone in his room, a gunshot was heard. Eastman had ended his own life at the age of seventy-eight. Beside his bed, he left a note:

To my friends

My work is done—

Why wait?

GE[16]

10

EPILOGUE

In the evening on March 14, 1932, the bold, black headline of the *Rochester Times-Union* newspaper declared "GEORGE EASTMAN IS DEAD; END COMES AT HOME HERE."[1] Audley Stewart, Eastman's personal physician, issued the following statement:

> Mr. Eastman died suddenly at 12:50 p.m. today. While it was generally known that he has been ill for several years, his condition recently had been such to give us all encouragement. He was apparently, however, in such a mental condition that he feared the worst. . . .[2]

Eastman's suicide was difficult for his friends to accept. Many of them did not understand how a man who had been so full of energy and accomplished so much could take his own life. Evidently,

George Eastman in his later years

Eastman thought that since he had no children, and had taken care of his obligations, there was nothing else left for him to do. He did not believe useless people should clutter up the world.[3]

Funeral

On Thursday, March 17, at 3:30 P.M., Eastman's funeral was held in St. Paul's Episcopal Church. Throughout the city, all activity was suspended at the hour of the funeral. Thousands of mourners lined the rain-soaked street leading to the church. Amplifiers were set up so the mourners outside the church could hear the service, which was broadcast nationwide by a local radio station.

Eastman's friends—Dr. Audley Stewart, Martin Johnson, Dr. Albert Kaiser, Charles F. Hutchison, Dr. Albert Chapman, and Dr. George Whipple—carried his coffin into the church. Reverend George Norton escorted the coffin down the aisle to the altar. During the service, Harold Gleason, Eastman's organist, played Eastman's favorite music.

At the end of the service, as Eastman's coffin was being carried from the church, Gleason began to play *March Romaine,* music from a German opera. Eastman had been particularly fond of the piece. It was not the kind of music normally heard at a funeral, but Eastman called it his funeral march. He had

George Eastman's flower-covered coffin is carried outside St. Paul's Church in Rochester, New York.

once remarked to Gleason after hearing it, "We'll giv'em hell when they carry me out the front door."[4]

Legacy

George Eastman was a shy, modest, practical man who had simplified the photographic process and made it accessible to everyone. He was also a tough businessman who believed in manufacturing "good goods," worldwide distribution of products, customer service, and fostering research. He was a pioneer in the area of employee relations. As a philanthropist, he put his vast fortune to work to support education, scientific research, and health care. His deeds touched the lives of millions around the world, and his name became synonymous with the word *photography*.

On the one-hundredth anniversary of George Eastman's birthday, July 7, 1954, the U.S. Post Office issued a stamp in Eastman's honor. During the ceremonics in Rochester on July 12, 1954, Marion B. Folsom, a Kodak employee who had known Eastman well and eventually became the Director of the Eastman Kodak Company, remarked:

> In his life, George Eastman, an unusually modest man, did not consider himself great. Nor did he seek fame—in fact, he avoided it. Yet he *was* great. And it is fitting . . . that our Government should honor him with a commemorative stamp in its series of Famous Americans.[5]

CHRONOLOGY

1854—Born in Waterville, New York, on July 12.

1860—Eastman family moves to Rochester, New York.

1862—Father, George Washington Eastman, dies on May 2.

1868—Hired by insurance agent as errand boy; Sister Ellen marries George Worthington Andrus.

1870—Goes to work for Buell & Brewster Insurance Company; Sister Katy Eastman dies on December 3.

1874—Hired as junior bookkeeper at the Rochester Savings Bank.

1877—Plans trip to Santo Domingo to investigate the possibility of buying land on the island; Purchases photographic equipment to document trip; Studies photography with two local photographers.

1878—Travels to Mackinac Island on Lake Huron in Michigan and photographs natural bridge; Experiments with dry-plate emulsions for photographic glass plates.

1879—Invents and patents plate-coating machine.

1880—Sets up his own business selling photographic dry plates.

1881—Establishes Eastman Dry-Plate Company and forms a partnership with Henry Strong in January; Resigns his position at the Rochester Savings Bank on September 5.

1884—Introduces new paper-backed film called stripping film and later American film; Invents, with the assistance of William Walker, a roller holder that advances film inside a camera; Sister Ellen dies.

1885—Patents roller holder and sends William Walker to London to establish branch office.

1886—Hires Henry Reichenbach, a chemist, to experiment with photographic emulsions and develop a lightweight transparent film.

1888—Places first camera on the market and invents the word *Kodak*, which eventually becomes his company's trademark.

1889—On a trip to Europe with his mother meets George and Josephine Dickman in July; Introduces lightweight transparent film in September and patents film in December; Supplies Thomas Edison with rolls of transparent film to use in his experiments with motion pictures.

1890—Breaks ground for first buildings at Kodak Park in Rochester, New York, in October.

1892—Fires Henry Reichenbach and several other employees who are involved in a conspiracy in January; Changes company's name to Eastman Kodak Company in May.

1893—Cuts salaries, including his own, 25 percent to survive bad times.

1894—Hires William Stuber.

1895—Wilhelm C. Röntgen discovers invisible electromagnetic energy he names X rays.

1898—George Dickman dies in London; Patent for transparent film issued to Reverend Hannibal Goodwin.

1899—Capitalizes Eastman Kodak Company in London and makes first million dollars; Pays employees a bonus called "divvy."

1900—Markets Brownie camera that sells for one dollar.

1901—Niece, Ellen Andrus, marries George Dryden of Cleveland.

1902—Donates money for the construction of science buildings at the University of Rochester; Begins construction on a new house located at 900 East Avenue in Rochester, New York.

1905—Entertains for the first time in new home.

1907—His mother, Maria Eastman, dies on June 16.

1911—U.S. government files an antitrust suit against Eastman Kodak Company.

1912—Pledges $2.5 million to MIT on the condition that his identity remain anonymous; Pays employees wage dividends for the first time in April.

1913—Court rules against Eastman Kodak Company in Goodwin lawsuit.

1914—Donates five thousand dollars to build veterinary hospital at Tuskegee Institute for African Americans; World War I begins in Europe.

1915—Court rules against Eastman Kodak Company in antitrust lawsuit on August 24.

1916—Donates five hundred thousand dollars to MIT, making his total donation $3 million; Josephine Dickman dies.

1917—The United States declares war on Germany in March; Establishes Alexander Street Clinic dental clinic in Rochester.

1918—Establishes school of aerial photography at Kodak Park in January.

1920—Establishes medical and dental school at University of Rochester, along with John D. Rockefeller; Returns profits he made on war contract to United States government.

1922—Establishes a school of music at the University of Rochester.

1925—Donates $30 million to MIT, Hampton Institute, Tuskegee Institute, and the University of Rochester on December 8; Retires from Eastman Kodak Company.

1926—Goes on a six-month safari in Africa.

1928—Goes on second safari in Africa.

1930—Celebrates the fiftieth anniversary of Eastman Kodak Company.

1932—Commits suicide on March 14.

CHAPTER NOTES

Chapter 1. Amateur

1. Elizabeth Brayer, "George Eastman," *Rochester History*, vol. LII, no. 1, Winter 1990, p. 4.

2. Roger Butterfield, "The Prodigious Life of George Eastman," *Life*, April 26, 1954, p. 156.

3. Carl Ackerman, *George Eastman* (New York: Houghton Mifflin Company, 1930), p. 25.

4. Ibid., p. 24.

5. Butterfield, p. 156.

6. Susan Adams, "As Convenient as a Pencil," *Forbes Magazine*, November 30, 1998, p. 400.

Chapter 2. Early Years

1. Elizabeth Brayer, *George Eastman: A Biography* (Baltimore, Md.: The Johns Hopkins University Press, 1996), p. 11.

2. Ibid., p. 13.

3. Ibid., p. 14.

4. Ibid., p. 15.

5. Ibid., p. 16.

6. Ibid., p. 17.

7. Ibid., p. 19.

8. Ibid., p. 20.

9. Ibid.

10. Ibid., p. 22.

11. Ibid., pp. 24–25.

12. Ibid., p. 25.

Chapter 3. Inventor

1. Carl Ackerman, *George Eastman* (New York: Houghton Mifflin Co., 1930), p. 26.

2. University of Rochester, Eastman-Butterfield Collection, Interview with L. S. Foulkes, D:4, 1:5.

3. Ackerman, p. 26.

4. Elizabeth Brayer, *George Eastman: A Biography* (Baltimore, Md.: The Johns Hopkins University Press, 1996), p. 32.

5. Ibid., p. 33.

6. Ibid., p. 36.

7. Ibid., p. 37.

8. Ibid., p. 40.

9. Ackerman, p. 43.

10. Ibid.

10. Brayer, p. 42.

11. "A Great Man," *University of Rochester Library Bulletin*, vol. 26, no. 3, Spring 1971, p. 65.

13. *The American Experience, The Wizard of Photography*, May 19, 2000, transcript p. 4.

14. Douglas Collins, *The Story of Kodak* (New York: Harry N. Abrams, Inc., 1945), p. 51.

15. Ackerman, p. 49.

16. Collins, p. 50.

Chapter 4. Businessman

1. Douglas Collins, *The Story of Kodak* (New York: Harry N. Abrams, Inc., 1945), p. 54.

2. Elizabeth Brayer, *George Eastman: A Biography* (Baltimore, Md.: The Johns Hopkins University Press, 1996), p. 49.

3. Carl Ackerman, *George Eastman* (New York: Houghton Mifflin Company, 1930), p. 57.

4. Brayer, p. 49

5. Collins, p. 66.

6. Ackerman, p. 55.

7. University of Rochester, Eastman-Butterfield Collection, Interview with Harry W. Fell, D:4, 1:5.

8. Eastman Kodak Company, *How Kodak Got Its Name* (Rochester, N.Y.: Eastman Kodak Company), p. 2.

9. Brayer, p. 66.

10. Ibid.

11. Collins, p. 59.

12. Ibid., pp. 59–60.

13. Eastman Kodak Company, *From Glass Plates to Digital Images . . .: The Kodak Story* (Rochester, N.Y.: Eastman Kodak Company, 1994), p. 7.

14. Collins, p. 65.

15. Brian Coe, *George Eastman and the Early Photographers* (London: Priory Press Ltd., 1973), pp. 70–71.

16. Collins, p. 68.

17. Ackerman, p. 66.

18. Brayer, p. 74.

19. Ibid., p. 73.

20. Ibid., p. 81.

21. Ibid., p. 124.

22. Ibid., p. 126.

23. Ibid., p. 77.

24. Ibid.

25. *The American Experience, The Wizard of Photography,* May 19, 2000, <http://www.pbs.org/wgbh/amex/Eastman/sfeature/music_yourpress.html.> (November 1, 2001)

26. Brayer, p. 89.

27. Roger Butterfield, "The Prodigious Life of George Eastman," *Life*, April 26, 1954, p. 154.

Chapter 5. Ups and Downs

1. Elizabeth Brayer, *George Eastman: A Biography* (Baltimore, Md.: The Johns Hopkins University Press, 1996), p. 92.

2. Carl Ackerman, *George Eastman* (New York: Houghton Mifflin Company, 1930), p. 105.

3. Ibid.

4. Brayer, p. 94.

5. Ibid., p. 144.

6. Ibid., p. 148.

7. "Reminiscences of George Eastman," *University of Rochester Library Bulletin*, vol. 26, no. 3, Spring 1971, p. 55.

8. Ackerman, p. 109.

9. Brayer, pp. 177–178.

10. Roger Butterfield, "The Prodigious Life of George Eastman," *Life*, April 26, 1954, p. 160.

11. Douglas Collins, *The Story of Kodak* (New York: Harry N. Abrams, Inc., 1945), p. 108.

12. George Eastman House, Eastman Collection, *Kodak Trade Circular*, September 1901.

13. Brayer, p. 162.

14. Ibid., p. 239.

Chapter 6. Millionaire

1. "George Eastman and the University of Rochester," *University of Rochester Library Bulletin*, vol. 26, no. 3, Spring 1971, p. 143.

2. Ibid., p. 142.

3. Elizabeth Brayer, "George Eastman," *Rochester History*, vol. LII, no. 1, Winter 1990, p. 3.

4. Ibid.

5. International Museum of Photography at George Eastman House, *The George Eastman House and Gardens* (Rochester, N.Y.: International Museum of Photography at George Eastman House, 1992), p. 36.

6. Elizabeth Brayer, *George Eastman: A Biography* (Baltimore, Md.: The Johns Hopkins University Press, 1996), p. 258.

7. Brayer, *George Eastman: A Biography*, p. 259.

8. Ibid., p. 195.

9. Ibid., p. 391.

10. Douglas Collins, *The Story of Kodak* (New York: Harry N. Abrams, Inc., 1945), p. 191.

11. George Eastman House, George Eastman Collection, Hanging files, *New York Times* article, 1920.

12. Brayer, *George Eastman: A Biography*, p. 388.

13. Carl Ackerman, *George Eastman* (New York: Houghton Mifflin Company, 1930), p. 280.

Chapter 7. Philanthropist

1. Martin Wooster, "George Eastman: America's Unknown Giant of Philanthropy," *Alternative in Philanthropy*, April 1997, <http://www.capitalresearch.org/ap/ap-0497.html> (August 31, 2000).

2. Ibid.

3. Elizabeth Brayer, *George Eastman: A Biography* (Baltimore, Md.: The Johns Hopkins University Press, 1996), p. 342.

4. Douglas Collins, *The Story of Kodak* (New York: Harry N. Abrams, Inc., 1945), p. 149.

5. Ibid., p. 150.

6. Ibid.

7. Ibid., p. 149.

8. Warren G. Harding, letter to George Eastman, February 7, 1922.

9. Warren G. Harding, letter to George Eastman, February 12, 1921.

Chapter 8. Medicine and Music

1. University of Rochester, Eastman-Butterfield Collection, Interview with Dr. Harvey J. Burkhart, D:4, 1:2.

2. Marion Gleason, "The George Eastman I Knew," *University of Rochester Library Bulletin*, vol. 27, no. 3, Spring 1971, p. 99.

3. "Please Play My Funeral March," *University of Rochester Library Bulletin*, vol. 26, no. 3, Spring 1971, p. 112.

4. Elizabeth Brayer, *George Eastman: A Biography* (Baltimore, Md.: The Johns Hopkins University Press, 1996), p. 443.

5. Roger Butterfield, "Reminiscences of George Eastman; An Introduction," *University of Rochester Library Bulletin*, vol. 26, no. 3, Spring 1971, p. 53.

6. Brayer, p. 443.

7. Ibid., pp. 443–444.

Chapter 9. Later Years

1. Elizabeth Brayer, *George Eastman: A Biography* (Baltimore, Md.: The Johns Hopkins University Press, 1996), p. 477.

2. Eastman Kodak Company, *From Glass Plates to Digital Images . . .: The Kodak Story* (Rochester, N.Y.: Eastman Kodak Company, 1994), p. 10.

3. Brayer, p. 498.

4. Jamie Miller, "The Complete George Eastman: Everything You Always Wanted to Know but Couldn't Find Out," Eastman Collection (hanging file), George Eastman House, March 16, 1976.

5. University of Rochester, Eastman-Butterfield Collection, Interview with Mrs. George H. Whipple, D 1, folder 1.11.

6. Osa Johnson, *I Married Adventure* (New York: J. B. Lippincott Co., 1940), pp. 297–298.

7. Ibid., p. 299.

8. "Eastman Lemon; or The Culinary Art of an Industrialist," *University of Rochester Library Bulletin*, vol. 26, no. 3, Spring 1971, p. 162.

9. Johnson, pp. 298–299.

10. Brayer, p. 489.

11. Ibid., p. 494.

12. Johnson, p. 307.

13. Brayer, p. 509.

14. "Kodak 50th Anniversary Cameras," *On Tour: News for Gallery, Garden and House Docents*, September 1996, p. 3.

15. Brayer, p. 510.

16. Roger Butterfield, "The Prodigious Life of George Eastman," *Life*, April 26, 1954, p. 168.

Chapter 10. Epilogue

1. "George Eastman Is Dead; End Comes at Home Here," *Rochester Times-Union*, March 14, 1932, vol. XL, no. 2, p. 1.

2. Ibid.

3. Elizabeth Brayer, *George Eastman: A Biography* (Baltimore, Md.: The Johns Hopkins University Press, 1996), p. 527.

4. "Please Play My Funeral March," *University of Rochester Library Bulletin*, vol. 26, no. 3, Spring 1971, p. 124.

5. "A Great Man," *University of Rochester Library Bulletin*, vol. 26, no. 3, Spring 1971, p. 79.

GLOSSARY

amateur—A person who does something for pleasure, not for money.

appeal—To make a request to a higher court for the rehearing or review of a legal case.

bandwagon—A popular, fashionable, or winning group, movement, or trend.

castor oil—A thick yellowish or colorless oil obtained from the beans of a tall, tropical plant, used as a lubricant.

collodion—A solution of nitrocellulose in ether and alcohol that is used in photography for covering plates with a thin film.

conservative—A person who is cautious and not inclined to take risks.

conspiracy—Secret planning to do something unlawful or wrong.

contraption—A device or machine regarded as strange.

defection—An abandonment of loyalty, duty, or principle.

dogfights—Combat between individual fighter planes at close quarters.

emulsion—A mixture of liquids that do not dissolve in each other.

exclusive—Not shared with others.

foreclose—Take away the right of a person who has mortgaged property to redeem that property.

formula—A clearly defined concept, plan, or method.

glycerin—A colorless, sweet, syrupy alcohol obtained from fats and oils and used as a solvent.

Gregorian calendar—The calendar now in use in the United States and most other countries, having twelve months and 365 days (366 in a leap year) per year.

incisive—Sharp, keen, and penetrating.

ingenious—Inventive or resourceful.

irreversible—Unable to be changed or repealed.

League of Nations A group formed in 1919 under the terms of the Treaty of Versailles at the end of World War I to promote cooperation among nations and maintain peace.

moron—A stupid or ignorant person.

nitrocellulose—A cotton-like substance made from cellulose treated with nitric and sulfuric acids.

obsolete—No longer useful.

paralysis—The state of being helpless; unable to take action.

paraphernalia—A collection of items used in some activity.

philanthropist—A person who loves mankind and works for its welfare, especially by giving sizable donations of money to worthy causes.

phonograph—An instrument that reproduces sounds.

polio—An acute, infectious disease that destroys nervous tissue in the spinal cord, causing fever and paralysis of various muscles.

reconnaissance—To investigate and seek out information about enemy positions.

rhetoric—The art of using words in speaking or writing to persuade or influence others.

savvy—Intelligent, sensible, or knowing.

scrutinize—Examine closely, inspect carefully.

statistician—An expert in numerical facts.

thermostats—Automatic devices for regulating temperature.

tourist—A person traveling for pleasure.

transparent—Easily seen through.

undesignated—Not assigned to any particular item.

X ray—Electromagnetic rays having an extremely short wavelength that can go through substances ordinary light cannot penetrate.

FURTHER READING

Brayer, Elizabeth. *George Eastman: A Biography*. Baltimore, Md.: Johns Hopkins University Press, 1996.

Czech, Kenneth P. *Snapshot*. Minneapolis: Lerner Publications, Co., 1996.

Dolan, Ellen M. *Thomas Alva Edison: Inventor*. Springfield, N.J.: Enslow Publishers, Inc., 1998.

Mitchell, Barbara. *Click! A Story About George Eastman*. Minneapolis: The Lerner Publishing Group, 1987.

Oxlade, Chris. *Learn About Cameras*. New York: Anness Publishing Company, Inc., 1997.

INTERNET ADDRESSES

Eastman Kodak Company. "George Eastman . . . The Man." *History of Kodak.* 1994–2001. <http://kodak.com/US/en/corp/aboutKodak/kodakHistory/eastman.shtml>.

"George Eastman House International Museum of Photography and Film." n.d. <http://www.eastman.org>.

PBS/WGBH. "The Wizard of Photography." *The American Experience.* 1999. <http://www.pbs.org/wgbh/amex/eastman>.

INDEX